California Jesus

A (Slightly) Irreverent Guide to the Golden State's
Christian Sects, Evangelists & Latter-Day Prophets

by Mike Marinacci

RONIN

Berkeley, CA

roninpub.com

California Jesus

by Mike Marinacci

California Jesus

Copyright 2016 by Mike Marinacci
ISBN: 978-1-57951-230-9

RONIN Publishing, Inc.
PO Box 3436
Oakland CA 94609
roninpub.com

Production:
    Editor: Beverly A. Potter, PhD
    Book Design: Beverly A. Potter, PhD
    Cover Design: Brian Groppe   bgdesign09@gmail.com

Distributed to the trade by **Publishers Group West**
Printed in the **United States of America**

Library of Congress Card Number: 2016941114
Photo credits:

    Page 61, *L.A. Daily News Negatives* (Collection 1387) UCLA Library Special Collections,
        Charles E. Young Research Library.
    Page 100 , Copyright (c) 2016 by Jimmy Akin. All Rights Reserved.
        Used by Permission. JimmyAkin.com

Table of Contents

Dedication

To the Rev. Dr. J. Gordon Melton
—a gentleman, a scholar, and a Christian.

Acknowledgements

Thanks to the following individuals and organizations for their invaluable help in producing this book: Beverly Potter (Ronin Publishing); Tom Diamant and Chris Strachwitz (Arhoolie Foundation); Glenn Gohr (Flower Pentecostal Heritage Center); Linda Brenner (Metropolitan Community Churches); Philip Aguilar and David Trotter (Set Free Ministries); John Kersey (Abbey of San Luigi); Julie Graham (UCLA Special Collections Library); Judith Rosenberg; Jack Boulware; Joy McCann; Jimmy Akin; and several individuals who wished to remain nameless.

Introduction

For over a century, California has enjoyed a reputation both nationally and globally as a stronghold of eccentricity—"the land of fruits and nuts," as one folk-saying describes the state.

The Golden State's oddness has never been more apparent than in the religious sects it has fostered. The "California cult," that homegrown stew of theological and social unorthodoxy, has long tickled popular imagination, and its manifestations have ranged from harmless groups dedicated to practices like nudism or veganism, to sects of ritual-murder and mass-suicide like the Manson Family or Peoples' Temple.

California's Christian groups have produced a colorful and bizarre array of leaders and devotees

Christianity on the Western Fringe

Somewhat lost in the shuffle of California's diverse spiritual culture have been the Christian missions, sects, and denominations that have emerged there. Perhaps less exotic in pedigree than many groups one might associate with indigenous California spirituality, the state's various native Christian evangelists and movements have been no less influential than their "New Age" or "Eastern" equivalents on world religion and culture, and have produced an equally colorful and bizarre array of leaders and devotees.

California has long been a destination for adventurers, dream-seekers, and misfits seeking to reinvent themselves on the edge of western civilization, and the Golden State's bearers of the Gospel reflect these unusual demographic and cultural factors in both their theologies and their evangelical methods. Far from Old World strongholds of religious orthodoxy, or Eastern American standards of propriety or decorum, the Christian ministries that settled in the state have distinguished themselves in the often-novel ways they interpreted the faith.

Pentecostalism, the noisy, fiery, "Spirit-filled" form of Christian worship that claims hundreds of millions of adherents worldwide, first emerged as an organized movement in California. So did the Spiritual Temple of Mt. Zion and the Kingdom of Yahweh: two sects that absorbed esoteric concepts and practices, and mixed them into their teachings and worship. Other groups, like the Children of God and the Set Free Ministries, adopted the unconventional speech, appearances, and lifestyles of hippies, surfers, outlaw bikers, and other countercultures, to more effectively bring such "rejected" folks the Good News.

Significantly, women, people of color, and gays—barred from ministry for much of Western Christian history—openly led large, influential Californian Christian movements. The teachings and practices of such figures as Aimee Semple McPherson, William Seymour, and Troy Perry reflect both their experiences as disempowered outsiders in mainstream religious and secular culture, and the freedom California's culture afforded them to pursue their missions.

The state that produced Hollywood and Silicon Valley gave its Christian movements electronic tools to reach far greater audiences than any evangelists had before. "Sister Aimee" and Harold Camping's radio-based ministries brought Pentecostal passion and Apocalyptic paranoia to a vast global listenership. Gene Scott and the Worldwide Church of God taught Adventist doctrines to TV viewers across the earth, and leveraged the medium to raise millions in tax-free donations. Wesley Swift's cassette-tape ministry created an underground network of easily-replicated and -transmitted magnetic-media decades before the Internet.

> *The state that produced Hollywood and Silicon Valley also gave its Christian movements a worldwide media presence*

Saints and Sinners

The stories of these individuals and groups are inspirational, cautionary, and comic.

The immense reach and high visibility of California's Christian evangelists and sects guaranteed close scrutiny of their doctrines and doings, many of which were found wanting. Like so many of their non-Christian equivalents, the Golden State's pastors, preachers, and missionaries were complex and tormented individuals whose passionate and idiosyncratic crusades reflected their sometimes-chaotic private lives, as well as the struggles of the troubled peoples to whom they ministered. Some were offbeat saints, and some were con-artists and criminals, but most were decidedly mixed bags of sanctity and sinfulness, who applied the Word as they understood it to both their lives and those of their flocks', with results ranging from holiness, to horror, to hilarity.

If this "(slightly) Irreverent" book seems to place undue emphasis on the controversies, scandals, and legal problems these individuals and groups endured, it is because such tales are as old as those of Saints Paul and Augustine—self-admitted sinners who appealed to God for strength, fought both popular opinion and their own demons in public, and then too often failed to triumph. More than one evangelist crossed over to the Dark Side during their lives; their stories are included here not only as informal biographies, but as warnings about where some non-orthodox teachings and practices can lead.

Legacies Sacred and Secular

The men, women, and groups profiled here reflect the colorful and diverse nature of the California's culture, and the creative fervor it inspires. Herein are tales of an Oakland-based African-American preacher who was crowned King of a multi-national Monarchy, as well as that of an eccentric pre-Gold Rush pastor and gadfly who had himself buried alive to test his faith. There are stories of two gay evangelists whose radically different ways of dealing with their sexuality influenced modern Christianity, and two "Catholic" churches that split from Rome to pursue distinctly dissimilar spiritual paths. And, of course, there are media celebrities: several pioneering radio- and TV-based evangelists whose idiosyncratic teachings and flamboyant styles won worldwide audiences, but whose poor personal judgments hobbled their ministries.

Their stories, as well as those of the others profiled in CALIFORNIA JESUS, are inspirational, cautionary, and comic. They are California's theological, evangelical, and ecclesiastic legacies to a faith and worldview 2,000 years old and two billion people strong, and their effects will long be felt in both the Christian and secular worlds.

May the Lord they served in their different ways grant them mercy, peace, and Memory Eternal.

1

William Monéy
& the New Testament Church

William Monéy was the great-granddaddy of all California Christian sectarians and mystic eccentrics. The founder of California's first indigenous Christian denomination, as well as the author of the first English-language book published in Los Angeles, the irascible, querulous Monéy argued and blustered his way into Golden State spiritual history as the original, quintessentially Californian religious crank.

What we know of him comes mostly from his few surviving writings, as well as from the reports of the mid-19th century Los Angeles press, and the recollections of early Anglo-Californios who crossed paths with this self-taught frontier eccentric and self-proclaimed religious prophet.

According to his own account, Monéy was born into a working-class Edinburgh, Scotland family in 1807. "By a singular circumstance," he said of his nativity, "I was born with four teeth and the likeness of a rainbow in my right

Money's tombstone in San Gabriel Cemetery.

Mike Marinacci

eye," as well as a veil
died a year later, and
mother as a preco-
natural history at
adding philosophy,
to his youthful scho-
however, forced him

"By a singular circumstance,
I was born with four teeth
and the likeness of a rainbow
in my right eye."

on his brow. His father
he was brought up by his
cious autodidact, studying
the age of seven, and soon
law, medicine, and theology
lastics. Family poverty,
into the workplace, and at

twelve he apprenticed with a Glasgow-area paper manufacturer.

Monéy endured Glaswegian factory life for five years. But he ached to travel and study "the religions of the Jews, Gentiles and Christians," and at seventeen he embarked on a voyage to the New World, landing in New York in 1825. While standing on a Manhattan street corner he heard the call to preach the Gospel, and decided that the Republic of Mexico cried out for his ministrations.

Monéy vs. Catholicism

The Gospel that Monéy preached, in keeping with the tenor of the times, was an ultra-Protestant one. Centuries of anti-Catholic feeling in the United Kingdom—particularly in Monéy's native Scotland—combined with fears of the increasing Catholic immigration to British and American shores, fed a rising tide of theological and political anti-Popery in the English-speaking world that deeply influenced the young evangelist. And Monéy's destination, Catholic-dominated Mexico, was beginning a century-long struggle over Church influence on its governance and culture.

Monéy first migrated to Mexico City, where he opened a small paper factory. Then he moved to the town of Piquito, Sonora, where in 1835 he began a series of public debates with seven different Franciscan friars about the nature and teachings of the Roman Catholic Church. Like so many other would-be reformers before and since, Monéy argued that the Church had lost its direction over the last fifteen centuries, and that it needed to jettison its dogma, ritual and hierarchism, and return to the first-century Christian community's simple evangelical approach and Bible-centered doctrines. According to Monéy:

These and other learned propositions were discussed and rediscussed, constantly for five years…. Time would not admit of detailing the shadow of what transpired during the session.

Suffice it to say that through the indomitable faith and energy of Mr. Monéy, his seven opponents were entirely overcome; one sickened early in the second year and was constrained to take a voyage by sea; two others died of hemorrhage of the lungs; one went crazy, two became converted and left the Council in the year 1838, and were found by Mr. Monéy to have entered into connubial bonds, and were in the enjoyment of perfect happiness. The other two strenuously held out up to the year 1840, when exhausted, sick and dismayed, the Council…was broke up by offering me money to give up my sword, the word of God, but [I] protested, saying God keep me from such treacherous men, and becoming a traitor to my God.

After triumphantly driving the Franciscan padres to defeat, exile, insanity, and death, Monéy traveled to the settlement of *El Pueblo de la Reyna de los Angeles*—today's Los Angeles—in Mexican *Alta California*. Home to around 2,000 Mexicans, Americans, and Europeans in 1840, Monéy found work there repairing the plaza church. He also used his cartographic skills to draw up a map of a proposed land grant for the wealthy Sepulveda family.

Downtown Los Angeles in Monéy's era

Monéy migrated between Los Angeles and Sonora throughout the 1840s. On one trip during the 1846 Bear Flag Revolt, General Stephen W. Kearny's US Army dragoons took Monéy and his Mexican wife Isabella prisoner as suspected enemy partisans. Monéy claimed that while he was in custody, Kearny's troops destroyed over 1,000 of his hand-drawn maps of the California territory, which John C. Fremont later said may have been the greatest collection of its kind in the United States, worth as much as $250,000. The Scots-Mexican-Californian sage tried to sue the US Government for compensation, but was rebuffed.

L.A.'s First English Book

By the time California had become American territory, Monéy had settled permanently in Los Angeles, and reinvented himself as a doctor and healer. The self-taught physician would later claim that in this career he had treated over 5,000 patients, only four of whom died under his care. Monéy also said that he'd written two full-length, illustrated medical books, although neither volume ever appeared in print. Eventually, faced with more educated and sophisticated competitors, as well as a litany of complaints about his conduct during a smallpox epidemic, Monéy abandoned the medical profession.

> *"I have been turned out of doors. I have been stricken by men's hands. I have suffered hunger, thirst, sickness, nakedness, imprisonment, [and] treated like a foolish man."*

The Scotsman then returned to his first intellectual love: Christian theology. In 1851, Monéy claimed, he wrote a massive theological work while visiting New York City. Titled *The Church of Rome Reformed*, the book earned him $300 advance money from a prospective publisher that he used to buy fare back to Los Angeles. Like his medical works, the volume—if it ever existed outside of Monéy's imagination—never appeared in print.

However, Monéy did manage to produce one tangible theological monograph: *Reform of the New Testament Church/Reforma de la Iglesia del Nuevo Testamento*. Appearing in 1854,

"Discontinue your struggles with a giant that can strangle you without exertion."

the 22-page booklet was printed in parallel columns of both English and Spanish, and is believed to be the first English-language tome published in Los Angeles.

The book appeared under the auspices of the "New Testament Church," whose council had chosen the author as Bishop, Deacon and Defender of the Faith, and had given him and his work "all dignified admiration." Along with his youthful studies in theology and other academic disciplines, the volume's *Curriculum Vitae* also boasted of the author's expertise in such subjects as, "Philosophy of Sound in a Conch shell, peculiar habits of the Muskrat, and the component parts of Swain's Vermifuge."

In the work, Monéy claimed a lifetime of suffering in defense of sound Christian doctrine: "I have been turned out of doors. I have been stricken by men's hands. I have suffered hunger, thirst, sickness, nakedness, imprisonment, [and] treated like a foolish man." He expected further calumny from not just the Church of Rome, but also from the

Monéy's angry letters appeared regularly in the Los Angeles Star.

Along with the Roman Catholic Church, William Monéy's prime ecclesiastic enemies were the Mormons, whom he saw not only as polygamy-practicing heretics, but as rivals in his quest to establish a "Reformed" Christian church in Southern California.

The Latter-Day Saints first arrived in Southern California in January 1847, at the tail end of the Mexican War. The "Mormon Battalion"—the only American military unit ever segregated by religion—landed in San Diego that month after a grueling, 2,000-mile march across the American Southwest.

With the war mostly over, the soldiers were assigned to regional peacekeeping duties, one of which was the construction of a fort near Cajon Pass to guard Mexican ranchos against bandits. The Battalion also established a supply-line between the region and the Mormon strongholds in Utah, sending much-needed cattle, cuttings, and supplies to the Salt Lake Valley in 1848.

Mormon Battalion, en route to California

George M. Ottinger

Hearing of the Southern California activities, Church President Brigham Young dispatched representatives to scope out the land for a possible Mormon colony. When they returned with glowing reports about the territory, Young authorized 437 Mormon men, women, and children to head West and establish a Church settlement there.

The settlers arrived in what is now San Bernardino in 1851. There, Mormon Battalion members brokered a deal to buy a 35,000-acre rancho, and that October the pioneers erected over 100 homes on the land—the first American settlement in the region since California entered the Union.

Weeks later, hearing reports of an imminent Indian attack, the settlers rearranged their crude cabins into a solid row, forming a 700 foot-long, twelve foot-high stockade manned by Mormon Battalion veterans. Fortunately for them, the local Cahuilla Indian chief suppressed the tribal renegades, and the pioneers went back to building cabins, breaking ground for farms, and creating a logging road to supply Los Angeles with lumber cut from the San Bernardino mountain forests.

Despite its sectarian roots, the San Bernardino Mormon colony was a haven of diversity and tolerance. Multicultural Mormon converts—White Southerners, freed Black slaves, Polynesian immigrants—worked together amicably in the settlement's sawmills and farms. Cahuilla and Serrano Indians freely mixed with the settlers, and Mexican ranchers and politicians befriended Latter Day Saints colony leaders. Several Jewish merchants also settled peacefully into the community.

The colony didn't last. Disputes over land, and pressures from an ever-growing, neighboring "Gentile"—non-Mormon—population, weakened the community. And in 1857, when the US government threatened to invade Utah, Brigham Young called home the Mormon diaspora to help defend the territory. By the end of the year, over two-thirds of the colony's 3,000 residents had sold or abandoned their properties, and the ones who remained were mostly absorbed into Gentile society.

Early California's great Mormon colony was no more. But the agricultural and economic infrastructure the Latter Day Saints established jump-started the Southland's development, and is a key to the region's religious and cultural history.

Eastern Orthodox and Protestant communions, saying, "I will not be astonished to hear from these denominations as soon as this work comes to light, because it will be against their own personal interest—that they will from the pulpits thunder against this work, according…their excommunications to all them that read this work, by the penalty of unpardonable pains of hell."

Monéy, however, reassured his readers that everything in the book was "the complete truth of eternity," and solidly based in Biblical research and interpretation. A true Christian, he said, would have no argument with any of his points.

In the slim volume, Monéy reiterated and expanded the arguments he'd made in front of the Sonoran padres nearly twenty years' earlier. Much in the style of Martin Luther, he made his case against Roman dogma, ritual, and hierarchy in a series of 52 articles, set out as theses and antitheses that contrasted the Primitive Christian Church against the modern-day Church of Rome. Article 1 set the general tone:

PRIMITIVE STATE

Article 1: The Primitive State of the Church of Rome in no where teaches us her infallibility.

ACTUAL STATE

The Actual State of the Church of Rome decrees that she is infallible; the Pope, Council General and the rest of the clergymen claim this infallibility, and none of them has got [sic] this from God….

Unfortunately, many of Monéy's arguments were clumsily written and poorly reasoned, and the book gained little attention. Only a small number of copies were printed, and today *Reform of the New Testament Church* is one of the rarest of all early-Californian tomes, with only two known surviving copies in existence.

Monéy's book found few readers, but he continued to bait Los Angeles' Catholic establishment in letters to local newspaper editors. His chief target was priest Fr. Anaclete Lestrade, who

The ruins of "The Monéyan Institute, 1895

refused a public debate with the would-be theologian, remarking that Angelenos thought of him as nothing more than "a crazy old man." The Bishops of San Gabriel and Monterey also weighed in against Monéy, with a follower of the latter warning him to "[d]iscontinue your struggles with a giant that can strangle you without exertion."

Monéy also argued passionately with the followers of another New World sectarian maverick: Joseph Smith. When he challenged Mormon Elder Parley P. Pratt to a debate about polygamy, the Latter-Day Saint, much like Fr. Lestrade, responded that Monéy was "out of his head, or *non sana menti*," and that his writings condemning plural marriage weren't worth addressing in a public forum. Eventually *The Star*, the Los Angeles paper that had hosted most of these controversies, tired of Monéy's endless tilting at ecclesiastical windmills, and banned the Californian contrarian from its pages.

"For the love of God, get me out!"

Buried Alive for Jesus

In 1855, Monéy made his other great mark in California history when he founded the state's first homegrown religious sect. He formally organized the Reformed New Testament Church in Los Angeles that October, naming one Ramon Corona as Bishop and claiming a following of eight men and four women—a sizable flock in a town of fewer than 3,000 inhabitants. Monéy aimed to evangelize Southern California through the church, and stressed the Bible-centered, apologetics-oriented aspect of his ministry, saying, "Miracles are for the ignorant and barbarous, who cannot be enlightened by arguments."

Yet Monéy was not immune to the lure of the supernatural and the sensational. According to one story, he once announced that he could be buried alive, and like Christ, arise from the grave after three days. When a skeptic bet Monéy that he couldn't do it, the evangelist procured a pine box, and was sealed inside it in front of a crowd of spectators. A grave was dug, the coffin was lowered into it, and dirt was shoveled onto the bier. When the reality of being buried alive hit Monéy, he panicked, kicking at the coffin and screaming wildly, "For the love of God, get me out!" Eventually he smashed open the coffin lid with his feet, and jumped hurriedly out of the grave, to the great amusement of the crowd.

Around this time, Monéy wrote a 300-page follow-up to *The Reform of the New Testament Church,* but once again a lack of funds and interest prevented it from being published. However, in 1859 he managed to produce *The Christian Church*—Los Angeles' first monthly periodical, which, like his book, appeared as an English-Spanish bilingual work. The few people who picked up the April 10, 1859 issue resisted his appeals to pay a then-outrageous five dollars for a years' worth of more Monéy jeremiads, and the monthly folded shortly thereafter.

Still, the failures and embarrassments didn't slow Monéy one whit. While he pastored his small sect, the self-styled polymath also combined his cartographic talents and his vivid imagination to produce a bizarre geographic theory he called the "Discovery of the Ocean." Monéy maintained that inside the Earth was a vast subterranean ocean, created by a hole in the North Pole that sucked in seawater. This interior ocean was dammed on all sides by fiery volcanic rock, which heated its waters, and then expelled the "Kuro Siwa" warm currents through another hole in the South Pole.

To illustrate his theory, he created a complex drawing of the Earth's hemispheres and the hidden sea within, and filed it with the Los Angeles County Archives in 1872. Monéy never completely explained the reasoning behind his theory, although historian J.M. Guinn said that the eccentric cartographer claimed that the Earth's fiery mantle had worn through most of the crust beneath San Francisco, and that the wicked city would soon collapse into a flaming caldera of lava.

A "Harmless Old Fanatic"

By 1880, the septuagenarian Monéy had withdrawn from public life, settling in the town of San Gabriel, north of Los Angeles. On a three-acre parcel there he constructed a bizarre edifice: two octagonal buildings of adobe and wood, linked by a gateway at the front of the property. Upon the gate were inscribed Greek, Latin, and Hebrew slogans, as well as ancient Assyrian cuneiform decorations. Behind it lay Monéy's oval-shaped main house and a small orchard. Locals dubbed the building "The Monéyan Institute."

Although the house contained a vast collection of books, manuscripts, charts, and mount- ed animals, Monéy himself was vir- tually penniless. When California his- torian Hubert Howe Bancroft visited Monéy in 1880, the ag- ing eccentric offered to sell Bancroft a big chunk of his possessions, as well as his memoirs, for $1,000. Bancroft turned him down—a terrible decision in retrospect, since Monéy's priceless collection of early Californiana vanished after his death.

"[He died] with an image of the Holy Virgin above his head, an articulated skeleton at his feet, and a well-worn copy of some Greek classic within reach of his hand."

Accounts disagree as to whether Monéy died in 1881 or 1890. His passing was as col- orful and enigmatic as his life; one report maintained that "the harmless old fanatic" died in one of the octagonal buildings "with an image of the Holy Virgin above his head, an articulated skeleton at his feet, and a well-worn copy of some Greek classic within reach of his hand."

Although he died a pauper, Monéy was buried in the Mulock family plot, in San Gabriel Cemetery. During his medical career, Monéy had treated young Dan Mulock after a boar gored him, and in gratitude, the prominent family gave him a final resting place. Today Monéy's grave sports the cemetery's strangest tombstone: a black granite marker inscribed with a picture of his octagonal buildings, and a legend that would surely have pleased the frontier polymath:

> **WILLIAM MONÉY**
>
> BORN 1807 SCOTLAND
> DECEASED CIRCA 1881 SAN GABRIEL
> PHYSICIAN—THEOLOGIAN—PHILOSOPHER—
> WRITER—NATURALIST—HISTORIAN
> ADVOCATE OF THE OCTAGONAL CONCEPT IN
> BUILDING DESIGN AND CONSTRUCTION

Although Monéy's life and writings intrigued early California historians, he has largely been forgotten today, save for occasional mentions of his doings in newspaper and magazine articles about famous Southland eccentrics. Still, he occupies a key place in Golden State cultural history, both for his pioneering literary efforts, and for the Reformed New Testament Church—the first of the countless homegrown sects that would mark California as a breeding group for idiosyncratic California missions.

2

William Seymour
& the Azusa Street Revival

Rev. William Seymour and wife Jennie, during the Azusa Street Revival

In 1906, a modest bungalow and a converted horse-stable in Los Angeles became the focal points of a spiritual movement that would sweep the Christian world, gain hundreds of millions of devoted followers, and split church leaders and theologians as to whether it constituted a genuine revival of the first Christians' evangelical fervor, or an emotive and dangerous mania that would lead believers into apostasy.

At the turn of the 20th-Century, Los Angeles was a far different city than the traffic-clogged, smog-shrouded, polyglot megalopolis of today. Boasting barely 200,000 residents, the city was still largely a mass of undeveloped subdivisions and orange groves, populated heavily with transplanted Midwesterners attracted by the region's endless-summer climate, scenic beauty, and cheap land. The oil industry was only beginning to tap the pools of crude that lay beneath the region's soil. The fledgling motion-picture business was still centered in New York;

the sleepy, conservative community called Hollywood wouldn't house a film studio until 1911. And the vast boulevards and freeways that would create and maintain L.A.'s automobile culture were decades away in the mostly carless city, where neighborhoods and suburbs were linked by hundreds of miles of electric-tram lines, rather than by asphalt roads.

At this time, around 5,000 African-Americans made Los Angeles their home. Most Black Angelenos lived in the downtown neighborhoods, especially the area around First and Los Angeles Streets—today's Little Tokyo.

Gift of Tongues

To this district arrived one William J. Seymour, a 35 year-old African-American preacher. Seymour, the one-eyed son of freed slaves, was a graduate of a Houston Bible school founded by the Rev. Charles Parham, a former Methodist who had embraced the revivalist "Holiness" movement. Parham's Bethel Bible College at Topeka, Kansas had been the scene of much excitement in Holiness circles when one of the school's class projects—investigating the nature of the "baptism in the Holy Spirit"—had resulted in virtually the entire class spontaneously uttering *glossolalia*—speech-like vocal sounds that believers asserted was identical to the Apostles' miraculous speaking of foreign languages at the first Pentecost. They called the phenomenon, "receiving the gift of tongues."

One of Parham's students, Agnes Ozman, prayed for and got the "tongues-attested baptism" on January 1, 1901. Significantly, the first day of the new century marked the first recorded time a Christian had consciously obtained such a power since Biblical days.

Enthused by what was happening in Parham's group, Seymour preached sermons at his own Houston-based Holiness Church about the phenomenon. Impressed, Neely Terry, a visiting Black Angeleno, invited the pastor to visit Julia Hutchins' Holiness Church at Ninth and Santa Fe Avenue, and share his preaching with her congregation.

Seymour arrived in Los Angeles on February 22, 1906, and spent the next few days at Hutchins' church, telling of the signs and wonders that were befalling believers in the American

"As people came in they would fall under God's power; and the whole city was stirred."

heartland. Alarmed by Seymour's talk, conservative church authorities locked him out of the church building on March 4th, but the preacher moved his mission to a parishioner's home at nearby 216 North Bonnie Brae Street, where he held informal Bible studies and prayer meetings.

For the next five weeks, Black and White Angelenos gathered at the Bonnie Bray house to listen to Seymour's preaching, study Scripture, and pray that they too could receive the same "baptism of the Holy Spirit" that their pastor's mentor had witnessed back in Kansas. Finally, on April 9th, one Edward S. Lee began to speak in tongues, followed by several other members of the group, including Jennie Lee, who would soon marry Seymour. The pastor himself received the "gift of tongues" on April 12th.

As many as 500 million people may be involved in Pentecostalism today.

Word of the phenomenon spread, and soon hundreds of Angeleno Christians of all races and social classes converged on the little Bonnie Brae bungalow. Huge, noisy crowds jammed the sidewalks and street around the house, praying, singing, shouting, moaning, and occasionally lapsing into glossolalia. Seymour and others preached to the crowds from the house's front porch, which eventually collapsed under the pressure of the throngs.

One neighbor described these open-air meetings:

They shouted three days and three nights. It was Easter season. The people came from everywhere. By the next morning there was no way of getting near the house. As people came in they would fall under God's power; and the whole city was stirred. They shouted until the foundation of the house gave way, but no one was hurt.

"Disgraceful Intermingling of Races"

With the meetings getting too big, loud, and boisterous for a private house, Seymour and his followers relocated to a dilapidated stable and former African Methodist Episcopal church at 312 Azusa Street. After clearing out the junk-strewn and fly-infested main room, and constructing improvised pews, the fledgling congregation started to conduct services three times a day, seven days a week as the "Apostolic Faith Mission," while Seymour and his new wife Jennie moved into lodgings on the building's second floor.

> *"The color line has been washed away in the Blood."*

Days after the Mission opened its doors, the great 1906 earthquake and fire devastated San Francisco. Believers were quick to connect the disasters to the Revival as signs that the End Times were at hand, and over 125,000 tracts were distributed telling of the apocalyptic events striking California. Soon, both Christian and secular periodicals reported the unprecedented goings-on at the little Los Angeles church, where as many as 1,500 people at a time would try to squeeze into the ramshackle building to sing, pray, and speak in tongues. Some were also "slain in the Spirit," collapsing on the dusty floor, their bodies twisting and flailing about—a phenomenon that soon earned Seymour and his followers the sobriquet, "Holy Rollers."

With the publicity, thousands of believers of all races converged on the Azusa Street building to receive the "Baptism in Spirit". Evangelist Frank Bartleman, who chronicled the events in his 1925 book, *How Pentecost Came to Los Angeles*, witnessed both the red-hot fervor and the incredible diversity of Seymour's fellowship, and made the classic observation: "The color line has been washed away in the Blood."

Other witnesses, however, weren't as charitable to the multiracial congregation. Although Los Angeles lacked the Jim Crow laws of the Southern states, it was still an informally segregated city where Blacks and Latinos mostly worked menial jobs, dwelt largely in downscale neighborhoods, and were generally expected to not mix freely or as equals with the White-majority population. Too, the fact that Seymour invited "sisters" to help run the services also raised eyebrows among Christians who'd taken to heart the Apostle Paul's warning to not let women speak in church.

Seeing Black, White, Latino, and Asian men and women not only worshipping, but ecstatically singing, speaking in tongues, and rolling on church floors together, along with women mounting the low podium to preach, alarmed many Angelenos, whose contempt and fear of the spiritual movement was expressed in a newspaper report of the time:

> *...[It is a] disgraceful intermingling of the races...they cry and make howling noises all day and into the night. They run, jump, shake all over, shout to the top of their voice, spin around in circles, fall out on the sawdust blanketed floor jerking, kicking and of them pass for hours as These peo- mentally de- They claim to They have Negro as their his knees much rolling all over it. Some out and do not move though they were dead. ple appear to be mad, ranged or under a spell. be filled with the spirit. a one eyed, illiterate, preacher who stays on of the time with his head hidden between the wooden milk crates. He doesn't talk very much but at times he can be heard shouting, 'Repent,' and he's supposed to be running the thing... They repeatedly sing the same song, 'The Comforter Has Come.'"*

> *[T]hey cry and make howling noises all day and into the night... These people appear to be mad, mentally deranged or under a spell.*

Other criticisms came from Seymour's fellow Christian pastors. Angeleno ministers warned their flocks against Seymour's church, saying that the preacher distorted Biblical doctrines, encouraged mass-hysteria among his followers, and short-changed the teachings of Christ in his lust to call down the Spirit. Some even tried to have the Azusa Street church shut down and condemned.

The Revival Goes Global

That September, the Mission began to publish a free monthly newspaper, *The Apostolic Faith.* Its first issue carried a front-page story titled, "Pentecost Has Come. Los Angeles Being Visited by a Revival of Bible Salvation and Pentecost as Recorded in the Book of Acts." That and successive issues featured eyewitness testimonies of Azusa Street's extraordinary revival, and were read by thousands of pastors and laypeople alike. At its peak in 1907, the paper was printing 40,000 copies per issue, and circulating all over the world.

Although thousands of people passed through 312 Azusa Street's doors over the next few years, Seymour's core group of local followers remained relatively small. Eventually the media lost interest, the crowds of curiosity-seekers left to pursue other sensations, and the Apostolic Faith Mission became just another congregation in Los Angeles' Black ghetto.

But Seymour's little church had scattered potent seeds throughout the Christian world, and those seeds began to take root and sprout in unlikely places. Missionaries who had visited Azusa Street took the revival to Africa, India, and China, where they reported that the "heathen" converts to the Faith were singing unaccompanied, speaking in tongues, and rolling in the ecstasy of the Spirit just as the Angelenos thousands of miles away had. Other evangelists spread news of Azusa Street across Europe and the Americas, and Christians of all denominations flocked to their meetings and revivals, bringing the enthusiasm back to their old churches, or starting new ones that carried on the spirit of the Los Angeles mission. Eventually the movement would be dubbed the Azusa Street Revival, and the emotive, ecstatic worship, and "Spirit-led" theology accompanying it would be called Pentecostalism.

Back in Los Angeles, there was trouble. When Charles Parham visited Azusa Street in late 1906, he was alarmed by what he saw as the fanaticism of the faithful, and distanced himself from Seymour's

A cartoon of the era illustrated the racist attitudes of many Azusa Street Revival critics

Brian M. Sandifer

church. Although his own ministry had reached out to African-Americans and Latinos, Parham also felt that the high-profile race-mixing in Los Angeles would lead to trouble, and condemned it as well.

Ultimately Parham maintained that formally organizing Pentecostalism would kill the spontaneous, grace-filled nature of the spirit-baptism experience, so he rejected his role as "Projector of the Apostolic Faith Movement," and left Los Angeles to continue to preach the Pentecostal Gospel. Allegations that Parham was homosexual—he was arrested in 1907 for "the commission of an unnatural offense"—dogged him for the rest of his career, and he died in relative obscurity in 1929.

With Parham gone, Seymour tried to wrest control of the rapidly-growing Pentecostal movement. But pre-World War I America wasn't ready to accept a Black leader of a multiracial Christian revival, and much of the religious and secular press of the time painted the Azusa Street movement as a dangerous pit of cultural—if not physical—miscegenation. On the home front, Seymour's 1911 feud with fellow Pentecostal preacher William Durham split the Los Angeles congregation, which had dwindled down to 50 or 60 mostly African-American faithful. Still, Seymour ministered to his Azusa Street flock until his death in 1922; today, he is considered one of the most important and influential figures in African-American religious history, and Pentecostalism remains a potent force in Black American Christian culture.

After Seymour's death, the Apostolic Faith Mission continued under the leadership of his wife Jennie until 1931, when the congregation lost the building's lease. Her death five years later marked the end of the Mission, but by then, Pentecostalism had spread to the farthest reaches of the earth, and had become the most powerful and vibrant movement in modern Christianity. As many as 500 million people—one-fourth of the world's Christian believers—may be involved in Pentecostalism today, and over a century after Seymour and his followers first received "the gift of tongues," the movement continues to grow worldwide. And it remains as controversial as ever among historical Christian denominations and orthodox theologians, many of whom see Pentecostal fervor as theologically unsound, psychologically destructive, and spiritually dangerous.

Today, Pentecostal faithful, religious historians, and sightseers alike still visit the little house at 216 North Bonnie Brae Street, where it all began way back on April 9, 1906. The house is now a combined museum and place of worship maintained by the Azusa Street Mission, which also offers tours of sites from the 1906 Los Angeles Revival. Although the Apostolic Faith Mission building was torn down in 1938, and the era's crowds of "Spirit-filled" believers have long since departed to their eternal rewards, the little Bonnie Brae bungalow stands as sort of Californian answer to *Acts'* Upper Room, where 2,000 years ago another group of seemingly ordinary men and women launched a worldwide spiritual revolution.

216 North Bonnie Brae Street, circa 1906

Enrichment Journal

3

Aimee Semple McPherson & the Foursquare Gospel

In 1907, the Azusa Street Revival reached across North America to the small town of Ingersoll, Ontario, Canada. There it captured the heart, mind, and soul of a teenage girl who would eventually relocate to Los Angeles, and become one of the Twentieth Century's most famous, colorful, and controversial Christian evangelists—Aimee Kennedy, later known to the world as Aimee Semple McPherson.

Raised a Methodist and a Salvation Army volunteer, the teenaged Aimee rebelled against her Christian upbringing and declared herself an atheist. The stinging rebukes Aimee received from her devout neighbors just encouraged her; she was a born performer who craved attention, and often spoke of one day shaking rural Ontario's dust off her shoes to pursue a career as an actress.

Yet when a tall, handsome Irish evangelist named Robert Semple hit town in late 1907, carrying the fire and fervor of Azusa Street

Aimee and Robert Semple, 1910

Pentecostalism with him, Aimee, intrigued by reports of strange behavior at his services, attended. There she saw men, women, and children alike collapse and throw *grand mal*-like seizures on the ground, babble in tongues, and scream and groan in a strange ecstasy. All the time, Semple seemed to silently fix his attention on her, as if to say, "This is the transforming power of the God you deny, Aimee. Repent now, and let Him guide your life."

And repent she did. Aimee gave up her dream of being an actress, and committed herself completely and unconditionally to Jesus. Although Semple left town soon after the revival, the Pentecostal fervor still burned brightly in Aimee's heart, and she ignored schoolwork, chores, and friends so that she could spend more time in prayer and meditation. Her parents were understandably alarmed.

One night, while praying over a sick woman in a snowbound house, Aimee suddenly and spontaneously received her Baptism of Fire. Here's how she described it:

> All at once my hands and arms began to tremble, gently at first, then more and more, until my whole body was atremble with the power of the Holy Spirit. Almost without my notice my body slipped to the floor, and I was lying under the power of God, but felt as though caught up and floating under the billowy clouds of glory. My lungs began to fill and heave under the power as the Comforter came in. The cords of my throat began to twitch—my chin to quiver, and then to shake violently. My tongue began to move up and down and sideways in my mouth. Unintelligible sounds as if from stammering lips and another tongue, spoken of in Isaiah 28:11, began to issue from my lips.

Shortly after this extraordinary experience, Robert Semple returned to Ingersoll, and proposed marriage to the 17-year-old convert. She gladly accepted, and the two married, and traveled on a missionary junket to China.

Missionary and Evangelist

For the next two years the Semples struggled to bring the Good News to *Heathen Asia*. Eventually both Aimee and Robert caught malaria; she fought her way back to health, but his case

Aimee Semple McPherson preaching at Angelus Temple.

gradually worsened, and he died in Macao. The day he expired, Aimee Semple was eight months pregnant with their daughter.

Ten weeks later, she left China with her newborn daughter, and eventually arrived in New York. Aimee's mother Minnie, who herself was doing missionary work with the Salvation Army, put her daughter and infant granddaughter up at her Manhattan apartment, but the arrangement quickly fell apart.

Feeling her daughter needed to be raised in a stable, two-parent household, she married accountant Harold McPherson after a whirlwind courtship. But soon after bearing him a son, Rolf, Aimee sunk into a deep depression. She refused to eat or sleep for several days, fell into a near-death state, and was placed in a hospital's critical ward. While there, she made a promise to God to leave her married life and "go out and preach the Word." Within a week, she recovered completely, checked out of the hospital, and left her children in Minnie's care. The revival trail beckoned.

Aimee separated from her husband (their divorce became final in 1921), and spent three years on the road, speaking at any tent meeting or evangelical camp that would have her. Audiences were astonished at the woman's vitality, stage presence, and sheer charisma; along with the usual Pentecostal phenomena, spontaneous healings sometimes occurred when Aimee chanced to lay her hands on an afflicted believer.

Tiring of the constant travel, Aimee landed in Southern California in 1918, seeking a permanent home. A region with a huge population of invalid and chronically ill people, the Southland was ripe for a revival by the attractive, compelling preacher who was by now making "healings" a regular

"I was lying under the power of God, but felt as though caught up and floating under the billowy clouds of glory."

part of her appearances, and she announced her arrival by blanketing San Diego with tracts dropped from an airplane. Thousands of people on crutches, wheelchairs, and even stretchers converged onto the converted boxing-arena where Aimee held forth; there, she spent hours praying over, and laying hands on, the afflicted multitudes until her strength gave out.

For the next few years, Aimee alternated her crusade between Southern California venues, and revival meetings across America. Although billing herself as an evangelist rather than a faith healer, the huge audiences that followed her at every turn demanded the same healing services she'd conducted in California, and she complied. As she crossed America, reports spread through the nation's press of the "miracle woman" whose revivals caused the blind to see, the lame to walk, and sinners to be reconciled to God.

Aimee called her ministry the Foursquare Gospel. The name derived from the prophet Ezekiel's vision of Man, Lion, Ox and Eagle, which Aimee took to symbolize "a complete Gospel for body, for soul, for spirit and eternity," and four cornerstones of a square, representing Regeneration, Baptism in the Spirit, Divine Healing, and the Second Coming. Although Aimee claimed the concept came to her in a 1922 vision, it's more likely that she borrowed it from famed British evangelist George Jeffrey, whom she'd worked with earlier in her career.

Evangelical Superstar

Flush with cash collected from "love offerings" at her revivals, Aimee spent a reported $1.5 million to erect Angelus Temple as a permanent home for her ministry. Located in Los Angeles' Echo Park district, the horseshoe-shaped temple boasted seating for 5,300 worshippers, two choir lofts for 100 singers, "the largest unsupported dome on the American continent," and eight huge stained-glass windows depicting the Life of Christ that Aimee herself had designed.

The Angelus Temple was dedicated on January 1, 1923. From that day on, it became the scene of a religious phenomenon unprecedented in American history, and the direct spiritual and conceptual ancestor of every gimmick-laden Evangelical crusade that's appeared in its wake.

The lady evangelist who'd once dreamed of stage stardom now commanded her own massive theater, performing three times a day, seven days a week, for an audience of thousands. And performances they were: elaborate, costumed, effects-heavy productions that more resembled director Cecil B. DeMille's Biblical film epics than tent-meeting revivals.

For one sermon, she donned a policewoman's uniform, mounted a large motorcycle, and sped the machine across the stage to within inches of the pulpit, where she jumped off, and, waving a gloved *"Stop! You're* hand at the audience, yelled, "Stop! You're speeding to hell!" At *speeding to hell!"* another sermon she decorated Angelus Temple in the gaudy bunting and tinsel of a carnival, and placed a working merry-go- round on stage, complete with children riding painted ponies. Still another production, "The March of the Martyrs," featured a procession of actors portraying St. Paul, Joan of Arc, and other historical figures, while Aimee hung suspended from an illuminated cross over the audience.

Aimee's preaching itself was equally revolutionary. Instead of the hellfire-and-damnation rhetoric that had characterized American Evangelical homiletics since Plymouth Rock, she preached a "Gospel of Reconciliation and Love," using anecdotes and affection, rather than threats of eternal torment, to reach her audience. "Let us lead them with kindness and sympathy," she advised her fellow ministers, anticipating the positive-thinking "New Evangelical" approach by decades.

Many of L.A.'s established ministers, who were losing followers to the upstart evangelist, criticized Aimee. They said that her feel-good theology was unscriptural and compromised her believers' commitment and faith, and that her stage-production revivals vulgarized the Christian Gospel. Aimee's defenders, including the noted *Nation* magazine writer Carey McWilliams, countered by saying her presentations gave Christians a sense of drama and pageantry in their faith, and were not that much different than the Medieval Church's "mystery plays."

But even the Medieval Church didn't go quite so far as Aimee did in turning Scripture into spectacle. One week she staged the story of Daniel in the lion's den, with a real lion roaring from the stage. Another time she built a giant whale onstage so that she could preach the tale of Jonah. To tell the story of Moses leading the children of Israel out of bondage, she created a replica Red Sea in the Temple with real seawater, and "parted" the waves effortlessly as fully-costumed Israelites fled a phalanx of Egyptian soldiers.

Many of these services were broadcast live on Angelus Temple's radio station, KFSG—Kall Four Square Gospel. Along with being the first important female evangelist of modern times, Aimee also became the first woman to obtain a broadcasting license from the FCC. "Sister Aimee," as her followers called her, would eventually control a network of 45 radio stations, and pioneer the concept of the electronic-media ministry.

When she wasn't holding forth at Angelus Temple, Aimee went on epic traveling revivals. On one 150-day tour, it was estimated that she traveled 15,000 miles and delivered 336 sermons to audiences of more than two million people. While she was on the road, her mother Minnie managed business at the Temple, and at the new Lighthouse of Foursquare Evangelism, a Bible college that would eventually produce over 4,000 graduates.

Disappearance, Kidnapping, and Scandal

By 1926, Aimee was at once a huge success, a genuine religious phenomenon, and a personal wreck. Years of 14-hour workdays, constant media attention, and running battles with her mother Minnie over Temple administration, had drained the 35 year-old evangelist.

Lonely and emotionally vulnerable, she walked into a scandal that electrified the nation, and stained her ministry for the rest of her life. For sheer audacity and notoriety, it would be unmatched in the history of American religious shenanigans until the Jim and Tammy Bakker follies of the 1980s.

The scandal began the afternoon of May 18, 1926, at Santa Monica's Ocean Park. Aimee and her secretary were sunbathing on the beach and working on a sermon, when suddenly the evangelist put down her notes and told her secretary that she was going for a short swim. The secretary paid her no mind until several minutes later, when she looked towards the waves, and Aimee was nowhere in sight.

"All who believe my story, say Amen!"

Although the secretary quickly summoned the lifeguards, they found no trace of the evangelist. Later a police airplane scanned the waters, but saw nothing. By late afternoon, it was assumed Aimee had drowned.

That evening, Aimee's mother Minnie took the stage at Angelus Temple, and broke the sad news to the assembled crowd. "We know she is with Jesus," Minnie proclaimed, and over 1,500 worshippers joined her in the Temple Bible School for an all-night prayer vigil.

The next day, newspaper headlines across America announced the tragedy. Crowds thronged the Ocean Park shores as motor boats and deep-sea divers—two of whom drowned during the search—trolled fruitlessly for traces of Aimee's body. And from Los Angeles to the farthest reaches of KFSG's signal, thousands of Aimee's followers mourned the loss of their spiritual leader.

All the while, the press and law enforcement were hearing strange rumors. One account had it that Aimee hadn't drowned at all, but had staged her own disappearance, fleeing her high-pressure life for parts unknown. Other stories had her kidnapped by rumrunners or underworld figures because of her campaigns against bootleg booze and dance halls.

The kidnapping theories gained traction when a note arrived at the Temple on May 25th that demanded $500,000 for Aimee's safe return, and specified a drop-off time and point for the money. Police staked out the area around the site at the given time, but nobody showed.

On June 2nd, another note appeared that named $25,000 as the price of Aimee's freedom. Two weeks later a third note arrived, with a lock of Aimee's auburn hair and an ante-upping demand for a $500,000 ransom.

Whoever posted the demand never collected the half-million. On June 23rd, Aimee resurfaced, alive and free, in the Mexican town of Agua Prieta. Brought over the border to Douglas, Arizona, she claimed that she had indeed been snatched off the beach at Santa Monica by hoodlums, and held for ransom. Her kidnappers, she said, had tortured her and threatened to sell her into sexual slavery. Finally, after being tied up and left in a remote shack, she escaped, and walked across the desert until she reached Agua Prieta.

Aimee returned to Los Angeles in triumph, seemingly resurrected just like her Savior. An estimated 50,000 well-wishers packed Union Station for her arrival, and when she said to them, "All who believe my story, say Amen!" they roared back in unison, "Amen! Praise be! Glory to God!"

Unfortunately for Aimee, the police didn't believe her story. Although Aimee claimed she'd wandered in the desert for over twelve hours after escaping, she was neither sunburned nor thirsty when she finally stumbled into Agua Prieta. She was unable to pinpoint the location of the shack where she claimed she'd been held. Nor could she describe her kidnappers in any real detail, or explain why she was wearing a watch when she emerged from captivity.

The Los Angeles Grand Jury convened

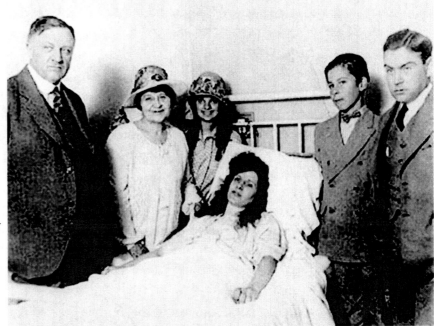

Sister Aimee, hospitalized in Douglas after her desert ordeal. L to R: L.A. District Attorney Asa Keyes; Aimee's mother Minnie; daughter Roberta; Aimee; son Rolf; Deputy D.A. Joseph Ryan.

to hear the confusing and contradictory accounts of the case. During the hearings, one name—Kenneth Ormiston—kept popping up. Ormiston, the tall, balding, erudite radio operator at KFSG, was rumored to be romantically involved with the fiery evangelist, who had been named as a co-respondent in his divorce. And two witnesses testified that Aimee and Ormiston hid out in a quiet Carmel love-nest between May 20th and 29th, while thousands of people mourned her death, and police expended countless man-hours chasing leads.

To the law, it looked as if the whole "kidnapping" was an elaborate hoax designed to give Aimee time and space for an adulterous fling, and she was charged with perjury. Several weeks later, after evidence surfaced that she and other Angelus Temple employees were trying to suborn witnesses and doctor evidence in the case, new charges of criminal conspiracy were added. But when the whole affair ended up in Superior Court on January 10, 1927, District Attorney Asa Keyes asked for and received a formal dismissal of the case. There was talk of a payoff, but although Keyes later served prison time for accepting bribes in an unrelated case, nothing could be proven.

Fading Star, Posthumous Legacy

Elated, Aimee mounted a "Victory Tour" across America in April, but her star was fading rapidly. Crowds were thinning, engagements were being cancelled, and donations were dropping off. While the State of California didn't try or convict her, American Public Opinion still found her guilty of adultery, deceit, and general hypocrisy—three deadly sins for a self-proclaimed evangelist.

Trouble was brewing on the home front as well. Mama Minnie publicly accused her daughter of mismanaging Temple finances, and several nasty quarrels between the two led to the elder Mrs. Kennedy's forced retirement. Angelus Temple might not have been bankrupt at the end of the 1920s, as Minnie claimed it was, but the scandals and management battles had drained its resources, and the revival spectacles were increasingly looking like Roaring Twenties frivolities. Aimee and the Temple battened down for the Depression.

Throughout the Thirties, Aimee and the Temple pressed on, albeit in far lower profile than before. Now committed to humanitarian work, her organization fed over 1.5 million hungry people during the lean times of the Depression. She still conducted services and revivals, but the garish stage productions and media sensations were things of the past.

The end came on September 27, 1944, when Aimee was in Oakland, California, a Foursquare stronghold where big crowds still turned out to greet the evangelist on her arrival. Although in failing health, she conducted a rousing service before retiring to her hotel room. Late that morning she fatally overdosed from sleeping tablets prescribed for a painful colon infection. Aimee was 53 years old.

Aimee lay in state for weeks at Angelus Temple, her bier visited by a reported 40,000 people. Tens of thousands more overflowed from the Temple during her memorial service on October 9th, which would have been her 54th birthday. A 1,000-car funeral cortege accompanied her body to Forest Lawn Cemetery.

To this day, Foursquare faithful maintain that Aimee told the truth about the kidnapping, and was unfairly maligned by the law and the media. The Foursquare Church itself has grown into one of the three largest and most influential Pentecostal groups on earth, claiming over 31,700 affiliated churches with more than 3.5 million members in 141 nations.

And Aimee herself is seen today as the quintessential Angeleno religious leader—a complex, fascinating character who combined Pentecostal revivalism with Hollywood showmanship, pioneered new roles for women in Christian evangelism, made the Gospel message palatable to modern audiences, and survived a scandal that would have destroyed lesser figures. Her spiritual and cultural influence will not soon wane.

Angelus Temple today

4

Bebe Patten
& the Christian Evangelical Churches

Adultery may have been Aimee Semple McPherson's downfall, but greed was the sin that spurred, and later crippled the ministry of one of her prime disciples: Bebe Harrison Patten, pastor of Oakland's Christian Evangelical Churches of America.

Bebe Patten emulating her mentor.

The Oakland Revival

The Oakland of 1944, where Sister Aimee's California crusade ended and Bebe's began, had grown into a major port and industrial city with more than 350,000 residents. Southern and Midwestern migrants streamed into the city to work in its burgeoning shipyards and defense plants, bringing with them the Evangelical fervor and Pentecostal passion of Bible-Belt Christianity, as well as a need for community and purpose in their new home. Too, their defense-plant jobs paid well, and many of these Dust-Bowl and Depression survivors suddenly had disposable income. Oakland was ripe for exploitation by any evangelist with the right pitch, and Bebe Patten stepped up to fill the role.

Like her mentor Sister Aimee, Bebe had heard the call to the Pentecostal ministry while still in her teens, and abandoned her dream of being an Olympic swimming champion to preach the Gospel. She then moved to Los Angeles, where she graduated from Aimee's LIFE Bible College, and then set off on the evangelical trail.

Although she had been raised in Detroit, Bebe was originally from Hickman County, Tennessee. On a trip back to her birthplace she met Carl Thomas Patten, a bootlegger's son and ne'er-do-well who'd just received a two-year suspended sentence for auto theft. Patten fell hard for the lady evangelist, and Bebe eventually agreed to marry him, but only if he joined her as a co-minister on the revival trail. Although he lacked formal education, he somehow got ordained by the Fundamental Ministerial Associa- tion, and became Bebe's evangelical partner.

"Green Palms! Choir Girls in White! Music! Miracles! Blessings! Healings!"

After nearly ten years on the Southern and Midwestern revival cir- cuits, the Pattens arrived in Oakland in 1944. There, they borrowed money from local pastors, assuring them they were merely in town to save a few hundred souls, guide them to established congregations, and then move on. Then they rented the old Elim Tabernacle church, and staged an extended revival for the Bay Area's heathens and backsliders.

Taking a cue from Sister Aimee, they publicized the revival with a media blitz. Carl, who was now calling himself "C. Thomas Patten," bought full-page newspaper ads, rented huge billboards, and sent sound trucks all over the East Bay blasting Bible verses at top volume, and promising spiritual spectacles at the Tabernacle: "Green Palms! Choir Girls in White! Music! Miracles! Blessings! Healings!" Patten later claimed his campaign singlehandedly "broke this town spiritually" on behalf of the Patten crusade.

The hype paid off. Crowds flocked to the Patten revival, which filled the 8,000-seat Oakland Arena on weekends. The campaign lasted nineteen weeks, and when it ended, in- stead of moving on to new missionary fields as they had promised, the Pattens took a lease on the 1,000-seat Oakland City Club, and settled down to pastor their flock.

Although she eschewed Sister Aimee's epic stage-spectacles, Bebe's services still copied her mentor's style. She wore white silk gowns onstage, led congregations in traditional hymns, and preached an emotionally-charged Pentecostal Gospel that left audiences drained.

While Bebe ran services and delivered sermons, hubby C. Thomas handled business affairs, taught classes, and most importantly, managed fundraisings—a duty for which he soon showed a distinct talent.

Bebe and husband C. Thomas Patten.

Flower Pentecostal Heritage Center

The City Club

In the fall of 1944, the Pattens bought the City Club for $265,000, nearly all of it raised from donations. When the Pattens' flock protested that the building housed a bar and dance hall on its second floor, C. Thomas said that the den of iniquity held a long-term lease on the space, and there was nothing they could do about it. In truth, the Pattens secretly cut a permanent-lease deal with the establishment's proprietors, and collected regular rental income from them.

Mr. Patten also promised that the building "will always belong to the people. It will be here until Jesus comes, until the hinges are rusted off the door....You will have it as a church long after my wife and I have left Oakland and have gone back to working in the field."

Soon, the Pattens started to style themselves not only as evangelists, but as educators. Both husband and wife obtained PhDs from the Temple Hall College and Seminary diploma-mill, and later bought the company's charter and mailing-lists. Calling their umbrella organization the Oakland Bible Institute, and their ministry the Christian Evangelical Churches of America, the Pattens established Patten College and Seminary, the Academy of Christian Education, and a music school for choristers. All were housed in the City Club offices.

"God gave me the power to take money from people."

Students at Patten College were mostly drawn from the congregation, came from all ages and races, and even included veterans on G.I. Bill scholarships. The College's 300-odd students wore navy-blue letterman's sweaters with huge, yellow "P"s on the front, took an eclectic variety of courses ranging from "Homiletics" to "Hawaiian Guitar," and staged noisy Friday afternoon evangelical pep rallies in the Institute's halls.

Still, the Pattens' worship services remained not only the spiritual, but the economic mainstay of their ministry. Held every evening, and three times on Sundays, the services always began with Bebe leading the congregation in high-powered Pentecostal hymns, prayers, and praises, whipping up enthusiasm and excitement. Then, she'd yield the stage to her husband for the real highlight of the service—the collections.

A big, florid-faced man with a roaring voice, who inevitably clad himself in gaudy suits, loud sport shirts, and cowboy boots, C. Thomas Patten mercilessly hectored the congregation for handouts. Often, he'd refuse to yield the floor for Bebe's sermon until the assembled crowd had coughed up enough cash. On the average, C. Thomas collected between one and four thousand dollars a service, but sometimes his "urgent appeals" could net much as $30,000—a considerable sum from a crowd of 1,000-odd blue-collar folks back in the 1940s.

"This is Where the Fireworks Start"

No American revivalist before Patten—and few since—worked the faithful for lucre as successfully, or as brazenly, as did he. His crude avarice and blatant bullying of his followers were virtually unprecedented in American religious history; the Western-garbed preacher gloried in his own greed, often telling people that his first initial stood for "Cash," and that "God gave me the power to take money from people."

At one collection service when donations were slow in coming, Patten ranted, "The Lord's not fooling around now. He's sick and tired of fooling around. He's going to hit somebody hard in a minute. He's just going to knock somebody flat." Frightened, his followers quickly passed along several fistfuls of bills to the preacher.

At another collection with disappointing returns, he bellowed at the congregation, "God is going to slap you cockeyed in about two minutes!" Then he narrowed his aim, knowing that someone in the audience would soon crack under the pressure: "This is where the fireworks start. God has been talking to one man for five minutes. I don't know whether he

Bebe greets her flock, while C. Thomas (seated on left) prepares to work them for donations

is going to knock him off his seat or not. God is going to…" Finally, when someone came through with a big offering, Patten shouted, "Bless you Jesus!" and the audience, perhaps relieved that they'd been spared more verbal bullying, echoed with "Amen!"

"God is going to slap you cockeyed in about two minutes!"

Patten often singled out members of the congregation for condemnation as cheapskates. He once called his own maid "the meanest woman in Oakland" when she withheld funds; scared and humiliated, she and her husband soon afterwards kicked in $2,800 to the ministry. Other Pattenites were so intimidated that they turned over most of their weekly paychecks to C. Thomas during the services.

One follower later commented on how the high-pressure collection tactics, coupled with the threat of damnation, so easily opened the congregations' pocketbooks: "All of a sudden, you had to make a choice—on the one hand, there was this thousand dollars you could give, and on the other hand there was Hell." To faithful Pentecostal Christians, the choice was clear, and they gladly forked over cash to save themselves from the wrath of God—not to mention that of C. Thomas Patten.

Patten mulcted monies not only from his unlettered, unsophisticated followers, but also from Oakland's most respected financial institutions. When he first put $8,000 down on the City Club property, Patten immediately used the deed as security on a $10,000 bank loan. In 1947 he convinced two banks to cut him $95,000 in totally unsecured loans, and another one to write $448,000 worth of loans in just one year. Patten wasn't always reliable about honoring his obligations, however; for several months, he successfully avoided payments on a $179,000 bank loan, and ran up nearly $3,000 of check overdrafts at the same institution.

To both his bankers and his followers, Patten always explained that he needed the monies for ambitious Church projects. There was his plan to build a super-Temple: a ten-story edifice topped with a 100-foot torch that would cast a Godly light onto the sinful Bay Area's darkest corners. Although he talked constantly of erecting this surreal synagogue, and purchased a prime piece of Oakland real estate for it, the property remained undeveloped.

"The Patten church meetings… are a racket dealing in hysteria, and a money-making device."

Another pet Patten project was the "orphanage." C. Thomas and Bebe bought 420 acres of land north of Oakland, and told their congregation that it would become a ranch and home for orphans. Generous followers donated enough money for them to buy a hardware store for building materials, and populate the ground with livestock, riding horses, and even peacocks. But the land was used as a recreational retreat for the Pattens, and they quietly sold it two years after its purchase, pocketing the proceeds.

Followers and financiers alike supported the Pattens' lavish private lifestyle. Bebe and C. Thomas lived in a mansion in Oakland's most exclusive district, and owned a fleet of nine luxury cars and a cabin cruiser. While Bebe clad herself in designer silk robes and silver fox wraps, her husband amassed a wardrobe of 75 suits, and over 200 pairs of cowboy boots. C. Thomas also dropped thousands of dollars at Reno gaming tables, and once stiffed a casino for $4,200 in gambling debts—a move that would have earned a lesser operator a severe beating, if not an early grave.

Revolt of the Sheep

The Pattens might have been able to fleece their flock indefinitely had they not made one fatal mistake in July 1947. That month, C. Thomas saw an opportunity to score a fast $200,000 profit, and sold the City Club building to the Moose Lodge for $450,000.

When the sale became news, Pattenites and outsiders alike howled in protest. Patten, who three years earlier had promised the building "will always belong to the people…until the hinges are rusted off the door," shot back, "It's nobody's business what my wife and I do with our property." When people in his congregation declaimed his broken promise, Patten held a special service where he threw huge wads of greenbacks onto the altar, and challenged his critics to come up and reclaim their cash. Immediately afterwards, he staged a high-pressure collection session, and most of the "returned" monies ended up right back in his pockets.

The Pattens were in trouble from other quarters as well. Following Sister Aimee's example, they tried to set up a radio ministry, and applied to the FCC for a license. An investigation revealed that Patten had systematically lied on the application about his background, criminal record, activities, assets, relationships, and pretty much everything else in his life. Not surprisingly, they were turned down for the license.

The couple had also worn out their welcome from their fellow religionists. At the FCC hearings, the Oakland Council of Churches testified against them, saying, "The Patten church meetings are highly emotional and hysterical. They are a racket dealing in hysteria, and a money-making device." C. Thomas brushed this off as mere jealousy: "All the other churches are mad because we cleaned them out. None of them get crowds like we do. We have stolen their sheep."

But by 1948, many of those "sheep" were finally wising up to the Pattens. The underhanded sales of the City Club and the "orphanage" property had become public knowledge around the Bay Area, and disillusioned faithful were complaining to the D.A. about C. Thomas' dirty dealings.

Finally, on November 4, 1949, C. Thomas Patten was called before a Grand Jury to answer various questions regarding his financial affairs. When he was asked if he believed in God, he took the Fifth Amendment—as he did for most of the next 100-odd questions about his doings. Shortly thereafter, he was indicted on ten counts of grand theft, fraud and embezzlement.

When C. Thomas came to trial on February 21, 1950, Bebe rallied the remaining Patten faithful, and scores of letter-sweater-clad Pattenites picketed the courthouse, and filled the courtroom seats.

Bebe and C. Thomas around the time of the trial

Flower Pentecostal Heritage Center

"I am the only man in the world who ever made a million dollars three times over from religion."

C. Thomas himself barely took the proceedings seriously. Throughout the trial he cracked jokes, told outrageous lies, and boasted that he'd actually taken several times the $691,000 he'd been charged with stealing. When cross-examined about his fundraising tactics, Patten offered to demonstrate them by working the jury and spectators for donations to his legal-defense fund.

"She is Praying in Hell Tonight"

During the trial, Assistant D.A. Cecil Mossbacher accused Bebe Patten of conspiring with her husband in all of his gambits, saying, "It was she who made the emotional appeal, she who set the stage upon which he operated…They conspired together to defraud and deceive this community."

Although she was never charged with any crime, during the trial Bebe revealed her uglier, vindictive side when she held a mock "sermon" over a pink rose taken from a disloyal ex-follower's funeral casket, saying, "This is just one of the many flowers that will come from the graves of those opposing us…Now [the dead woman] has no power to change God's word; she is praying in Hell tonight."

In the middle of the trial, C. Thomas suffered a heart attack, and had to be wheeled in on a gurney for the duration. According to one journalist, the silk pajama-clad Patten "listened to closing arguments from a stretcher, picking his nose moodily and getting an occasional shot of morphine from a hovering nurse."

The bedridden evangelist was found guilty of five counts of grand theft, and sentenced to seven years in prison. Much of the money he mulcted from his followers was never accounted for, and written off as gambling and investment losses.

After three years in the State pen, C. Thomas earned an early release because of his heart condition. However, his parole terms forbade him to ever perform another fundraising. The man who had deposited over $1.3 million into his personal bank accounts during the City Club years, and who had bragged, "I am the only man in the world who ever made a million dollars three times over from religion," retreated into the shadows of wife Bebe's ministry, dying in 1958.

With C. Thomas gone, Bebe began a long journey back to respectability, as a legitimate Pentecostal minister and revivalist. In 1960 she resettled her ministry, as well as the educational institute now called Patten University, on a five-acre site in Oakland's Fruitvale district, and spent the next five decades turning the school into an accredited and recognized Christian college.

Along the way Bebe cultivated many influential political connections. A lifelong advocate of racial equality who had long enjoyed a cordial relationship with Oakland's African-American community, she attended the funeral service of Dr. Martin Luther King in 1968. Ten years later, California Governor Jerry Brown spoke at the University, in support of a city-beautification project sponsored by the school. Bebe and the University also received three separate commendations from the California State Senate, as well as one from Oakland's powerful mayor, Elihu Harris.

Bebe died at 90 in 2004, and never lived to see what might have been Patten University's greatest coup. On February 1, 2008, Senator Ted Kennedy spoke before a crowd of 1,500 people at the school to support then-Senator Barack Obama's presidential bid. That neither the Democratic Party organizers, nor the assembled media there, seemed to be aware of the institution's checkered past, was mute testimony to Bebe's reformation efforts, as well as to the healing powers of time and forgetfulness. The scandals of six decades earlier remained a footnote in the histories of both the Patten legacy and Californian Pentecostalism.

5

King Louis Narcisse & the Mount Zion Spiritual Temple

His Grace, King Louis H. Narcisse.

Chris Stratchwitz/Arhoolie Foundation

Oakland, California's own self-crowned Monarch was "King Louis" Narcisse, whose temporal and spiritual kingdoms encompassed thousands of followers around the Bay Area, a radio-listening audience of over a million people across America, and a multi-million dollar network of businesses and properties he controlled as a one-man Corporation Sole. For over forty years he used his talents as a spiritual leader, gospel singer, and entrepreneur to build one of the most colorful and vibrant of all California-based religious communities, and one of America's most distinctive and eclectic African-American sects.

The Mount Zion Spiritual Temple

Like so many other self-made Californian religious figures, the future King came from humble and obscure origins. He was born Louis Herbert Narcisse on April 27, 1921, into a dirt-poor Black family living just outside of New Orleans, Louisiana. From an early age he'd been drawn to both music and Christianity, and later claimed that while developing his talent as a gospel singer in 1939, he'd heard the call to the ministry—a call he would soon answer faithfully and forcefully.

When World War II hit, Narcisse, like thousands of other African-Americans, fled Jim Crow-era Louisiana to work in the burgeoning San Francisco shipyards. By 1945 he'd saved enough money to open a church in West Oakland—a modest storefront affair with 50 folding chairs and a pulpit. Narcisse named his ministry *The Mount Zion Spiritual Temple*.

> *"A blessed nickel from God will go farther than a $1,000 bill with a curse on it."*

For the next ten years, Narcisse built a following among Oakland's burgeoning African-American population, most of whom—like him—were recent Deep South migrants whose social lives revolved around a church community. Along with holding Sunday services, every Monday morning he distributed "blessed bread" to poor and hungry Oaklanders from his house on 31st Street. The Reverend also counseled his flock on personal and business matters, steering them away from nearby Emeryville's card tables and San Francisco's nightclubs, and urging them to live sober, thrifty, and holy lives.

In a July 1963 *Ebony* magazine article, Narcisse told journalist Louie Robinson that he taught four foundational doctrines to his people:

First I teach the Sixth Chapter of Ephesians: honor thy father and mother. Second, I teach people to put on the whole armor of God. Third, I teach do good—whether people accept or reject you, they cannot change the good deed. Fourth, I teach the benefit of blessings. A blessed nickel from God will go farther than a $1,000 bill with a curse on it, or even one without a curse.

Cover for a CD compilation of King Louis Narcisse's Gospel recordings.

Often King Louis used the motto, "It's Nice to Be Nice" to sum up Temple teachings. To better express this sentiment of inner peace through kindness, he composed, sang, and recorded a gospel hymn with this title that became the unofficial anthem of his ministry.

A Joyful Noise to the Lord

Gospel music—an important part of the Black Christian experience—was a key element of Narcisse's Temple. Blessed with a rich, powerful tenor voice, the Reverend recorded several albums of both traditional Christian spirituals and original music during the 1950s. Although most of these recordings were released on fly-by-night labels, and had little commercial impact, Narcisse's talent and charisma caught the attention of such legendary figures as gospel singer Mahalia Jackson and rocker-turned-minister "Little Richard" Penniman, both of whom lodged with the Reverend when they journeyed to the Bay Area. And every Sunday, Narcisse and his choir's "joyful noise to the Lord" attracted ever-growing crowds to the Temple, many of whom came for the music and stayed for the preaching.

Unlike other African-American Christian leaders, whose theologies and sects followed traditional denominational lines, Narcisse' ministry reflected the eclectic spirituality and culture of the New Orleans milieu where he'd been born and raised. From the Black Baptist tradition he took the primacy of gospel music, full-immersion baptism, and the born-again experience, and added them to his church's practices. He also adopted the hierarchical structure and elaborate vestments of Roman Catholicism, and garbed himself in a bishop's silk robes and miter, his lieutenants in priests' cassocks and birettas, and his devoted female followers in nuns' white habits. And his Temple services, where men, women, and children chanted, clapped, danced, and collapsed to the floor from exhaustion, had the passion and ecstasy of Pentecostalism.

Some observers maintained that the emotionally-charged services owed as much to a fourth New Orleans religious tradition—Voodoo—as they did to any manifestation of the Holy Ghost. They noted that Narcisse had named his mission a "Spiritual Temple" rather than a Christian Church, lavishly decorated the Temple with colorful devotional candles and statuary, burned incense to drive off "evil spirits", and charged money—often up to $500—to anoint and bless holy water and oils—all practices more reminiscent of African folk-religion than Christian usages. Narcisse himself had often claimed to be the reincarnation of an African king, who had returned to lead an oppressed people back to God and grace.

King of the West Coast

Already the self-proclaimed Bishop of his sect, Narcisse's claims of royal authority blossomed in September 1955, when he was crowned "His Grace, the King of the Spiritual Church of the West Coast" by the Rt. Rev. Frank Rancifer at Oakland's Municipal Auditorium. From that day on his miter was a Crown, and he was King Louis Narcisse to both his followers and the world at large.

Influenced by the pomp and power of both Old Testament monarchies and the British Empire, he initiated his most loyal and generous followers as Princes, Princesses, Bishops, Lords, Ladies, and Queen Mothers, and took them on as his Royal Court to assist and advise him in his ministry. Untitled subjects tithed handsomely to the Kingdom as well, although not always without duress; one account claimed that King Louis would lock the Temple doors at his Sunday services—sometimes, past midnight—until collection plates were heaping with bills.

With his fortunes and influence growing, King Louis organized his Temple and Kingdom as a *corporation sole*—a little-known legal entity that allows an individual to control a religious corporation solely.

"[A] carnal man you attract with carnal things, and a spiritual man you attract with spiritual things."

Not only did this protect the Temple from the political squabbles and schisms that wracked other denominations, but it gave the King complete control over the Temple's real estate and property, allowed him to operate the sect without bylaws or a Board of Directors, and empowered him to pass the corporation on to a single designated successor.

Freed from the legal and organizational headaches of more conventional religious groups, and flush with offerings from his flock and income from tax-free properties, King Louis lived his regal title to the hilt. He established a 24-room "palace" in Piedmont—"the Beverly Hills of Oakland"—staffed with two secretaries, two housekeepers, a nurse, and a liveried chauffeur who drove and maintained a gold-plated Cadillac, a Rolls-Royce Phantom, and a Bentley limousine. When King Louis arrived at Temple services, his entourage would lead the crowned, silk robe-clad, bejeweled Monarch down a 30-foot

Chris Stratchwitz/Arhoolie Foundation

King Louis with the Mount Zion Spiritual Temple choir.

maroon carpet to the doors of the building, where the faithful would salute him, kiss the gold rings on his right hand, and sing tribute as he took his throne on the podium.

Criticized by some for his show of wealth in a poor, struggling community, King Louis responded in the *Ebony* magazine article. "I have built a solid foundation here at Mount Zion. I have labored hard, made sacrifices, and suffered," he told Louie Robinson. "The diamond rings, the flashy cars, and what have you attract attention. I'm not saying they are a gag. They were given to me by God. But a carnal man you attract with carnal things, and a spiritual man you attract with spiritual things." To King Louis, both kinds were welcome in his Temple, and he maintained that his gaudy display of riches inspired African-Americans to abandon material and spiritual poverty, and embrace the prosperity promised in both this world, and the Hereafter.

To the 300-odd faithful who packed the Temple every Sunday, King Louis was both a heroic monarch, and a spiritual avatar who inspired the passionate worship that Louie Robinson described in his article:

The flock is primed for the main event with services conducted by temple functionaries before the King arrives. Shortly after his grand entrance, he heightens the mood by leading the congregation in song with his rather pleasant tenor voice. Then he gets down to the business at hand: "The Lord is good. He is a good God..." Narcisse advises. "Sometimes the load is heavy, and the way seems dark and dreary... If you haven't got a mother, He's your mother. If you need a doctor, He's your doctor. If you need a lawyer..."

A woman in the audience gets up and begins pacing jerkily back and forth. Others rise and shout. A teenage girl screams, faints, is revived, and dances up and down until she collapses from exhaustion. A young boy in a choir robe begins a marathon race around the temple. A 40 year-old man dissolves in tears. Aging, enormous women scream and jerk about the room.

Soon the Temple became a mass of "singing, shouting, screaming, writhing, jerking, convulsing men, women, and children," all accompanied by a chanting and hand-clapping choir, an amplified R&B groove from the house band, and of course, the King himself witnessing and testifying to the Lord at top volume. At the ceremony's climax, the ecsatic, exhausted worshippers filled the collection plates, after which the King dismissed his flock with his blessings and prayers.

During the 1960s, King Louis expanded his Kingdom far beyond the Oakland city limits. Now a player in Bay Area politics, the King counseled San Francisco Mayor George Christopher in the City's historical-met with local police African-American neigh-his home town of New struggle, and donated *King Louis claimed to have two million followers worldwide.* about urban redevelopment ly-Black Fillmore district, and chiefs to help defuse tensions in borhoods. He also traveled to Orleans during the Civil Rights food and money to followers fighting Southern segregation and racism. And he led a fifteen-car motorcade across America to attend the inauguration of President John F. Kennedy; when he arrived in Washington D.C., local cops thought he was an African potentate.

King Louis also planted new Temple branches across America. California ministries appeared in Richmond, Pittsburg, Vallejo, Bakersfield, and Sacramento, and the Temple established Southern missions in New Orleans and Houston, Texas. The King also purchased a forty-room mansion in Detroit to house him and his entourage during visits in the Eastern USA, with nearby Mount Zion St. Peter's Chapel to serve as a place of worship. The Chapel sported a large picture of King Narcisse at the pulpit to serve in his absence from the building, with the caption:

> *God is great and greatly to be praised in the sovereign state of Michigan in the Kind of "His Grace King" Louis H. Narcisse, DD, where "it's nice to be nice, and real nice to let others know that we are nice."*

At the Temple's height King Louis claimed to have two million followers worldwide, with overseas flocks in France, Sweden, and Africa. Although that figure was probably a bit of royal hyperbole, the King's radio show, *Moments of Meditation*, reached over a million listeners across North America. Observers compared the Oakland monarch to such self-made, famed, and flamboyant African-American religious leaders as New York's Father Divine, Detroit's Prophet Jones, and Boston's Daddy Grace—comparisons that flattered King Louis, who saw those figures as his ministry's main influences and forerunners.

Decline and Fall

But by the 1970s, King Louis' empire was declining. When he tried to buy KDIA, a San Francisco-based radio station that catered to the Bay Area's Black community, well-connected local politicians aced him out of the deal. Critics accused King Louis of defrauding his followers and finagling Temple bank accounts. Persistent rumors that the middle-aged bachelor King was gay spoiled his relationships with more conservative Oaklanders—particularly those with children. And a series of tax disputes with the US government forced him to sell off his real estate holdings, including properties in California's Central Valley where he had planned to form a self-sustaining community for his followers. Although he still boasted a sizable flock, and hosted city officials at his public "Prayer Day" every March 9th in Oakland, his influence was fading fast as new religious and cultural figures elbowed King Louis out of the spotlight.

Finally, on February 3, 1989, the 67 year-old self-styled monarch and religious leader suffered a fatal heart attack in his Detroit home. His body was flown back to the Oakland Temple for a lavish funeral, where a host of his fellow ministers and over 1,500 mourners paid their respects to the King, laid out in an open coffin and clad in a pearl-encrusted miter, a fur-trimmed red brocade cape, white satin robes, and gold-mesh cowboy boots. An antique, horse-driven hearse took his bronze casket on a seventeen-mile journey up San Pablo Avenue to Richmond's Rolling Hills Memorial Park, where he was buried.

The King was dead, but no new monarch arose to take his place. Although he had appointed a brace of Princes and Princesses during his reign, King Louis had no legal heir nor designated successor. Claimants to the King's ecclesiastical and business empires from California to Michigan fought over his estate, draining Temple assets in legal battles and liquidations. Mysterious fires gutted both the Oakland Temple and the Detroit "palace." And several would-be successors to Louis' throne and altar battled for years over his title and legacy, with no resolution or clear victor.

Little remains today of Louis Narcisse's Temple and Kingdom. El Cerrito's Arhoolie Foundation has compiled a documentary, *Down Home Music*, that includes a six-minute clip of King Louis' preaching and singing during a 1963 service. And the KLHN Foundation, an online archive of his teachings and documents, preserves memories from the faithful who remember the lively Sunday services and the good works. But no current ministry in Oakland or anywhere else has carried on—much less duplicated—his singular apostleship. In all likelihood, his throne will be empty for many years to come.

6

Joe Jeffers & the Kingdom of Yahweh

Although he began his seven-decade career in the American South, and ended it in the Southwest, Kingdom of Yahweh founder Joseph D. Jeffers reached his peak of infamy during his dozen years in Los Angeles, and became one of the city's most controversial spiritual leaders.

The son of a rail worker, Jeffers was born in 1898 in Alabama. At twenty, he was ordained as a Baptist pastor, and became a disciple of J. Frank Norris, a Fundamentalist preacher who ran America's first radio ministry, and thundered against Roman Catholicism, liberalism, and evolution from his electronic pulpit.

During the 1920s Jeffers gained a reputation throughout the American South's revival circuit as both a spellbinding preacher, and a combative fundamentalist whose rowdy camp-meetings often ended in fistfights and arrests. Jeffers was especially fervent during the 1928 Presidential campaign, when he warned his Southern Protestant audiences

Joseph D. Jeffers

that Catholic Democratic candidate Al Smith was scheming to turn America's government over to the Vatican, and install *Negroes* as Federal overlords of White Dixie.

The Jonesboro War

In 1931 Jeffers started an actual religious war, complete with gun battles, in Jonesboro, Arkansas. Rebuffed when he attempted to take over the local Baptist Church a year earlier, Jeffers returned with an army of supporters, told them the Apocalypse was at hand, and led them in a riot against the pastor, as well as the Jonesboro mayor and police chief.

Alarmed, Arkansas Governor Harvey Parnell sent a company of National Guard troops and a military observation plane to quash the violence. Two days after they were withdrawn, someone bombed Jeffers' tent with a tear-gas grenade. Five weeks later, the structure burned to the ground.

In early 1932 Jeffers and his loyalists constructed a rival Jonesboro Baptist Church building, but he soon quarreled with his lieutenant Dale Crowley over who would pastor the congregation. For weeks thereafter Jeffers and Crowley held opposing, side-by-services in the church, where the rival pastors preached separate sermons, competing choirs tried to drown each other out, and shotgun-toting partisans scuffled in the pews.

When a court ruled in favor of Crowley, he and bodyguard L.H. Kayre armed themselves and attempted to take control of the church building. As they approached, Jeffers' watchman J. P. McMurdo opened fire on the men, wounding Kayre. When Crowley fired back, he hit McMurdo three times, killing him. The Baptist pastor was soon arrested and charged with murder.

While Crowley was imprisoned in the county jail, someone poked a submachine gun into his cell, and sprayed the room with bullets; miraculously, none found their target. Eventually, Crowley was acquitted of murder, although nobody was ever charged for the bombing, arson, or machine-gun attack. The Jonesboro War landed Jeffers in the pages of *TIME* magazine and national newspapers—the first of several major scandals the outspoken preacher would endure.

F.J. McCarthy & Co.

The Arkansas National Guard was called out during the Jonesboro War.

Yahweh in L.A.

Around this time Jeffers ditched Fundamentalist Baptism for what was known as "Sacred Name" theology. Originating largely in the Adventist movement, Sacred Name scholars believed that when one prayed to "God," one was addressing a generic deity, not the *Elohim* of Israel whose exclusive worship was mandated by the Bible. Similarly, "Jesus" and "Christ" were both Greek Pagan terms that misrepresented and insulted the Savior. Sacred Name adherents maintained that the Father and Son had to be addressed in their original Aramaic titles, *Yahweh* and *Yashua*, by true Bible believers, although they often disagreed on these names' exact spellings and pronunciations.

In 1935, Jeffers founded *The Kingdom of Yahweh* to spread his own version of Sacred Name woship. Two years later he divorced his first wife, and relocated to Los Angeles, where he preached the worship of Yahweh and Yashua to thousands of Angelenos at the Embassy Auditorium. Soon Jeffers opened his own church, the Kingdom Temple, two blocks away at 927 South Flower Street, and broadcast sermons over stations KMPC and KGER to a nationwide audience.

Nazis and Sex Scandals

Jeffers soon became one of the city's most infamous preachers—an eccentric L.A. cult-leader straight out of the pages of Nathanael West's period novel, *The Day of the Locust*. He bashed the Roman Catholic Church from the pulpit, claiming that "The Black Pope has had his hands in the political affairs here… but that is going to be changed."

Jeffers also decried the "Communist Jews who are trying to get a war with America," as well as the Jewish-dominated mo-tion-picture business, which he claimed was corrupting public morality.

> *"The Black Pope has had his hands in the political affairs here… but that is going to be changed."*

His rhetoric caught the attention of the House Un-American Activities Committee in Washington, DC. Congressional investi-gators found out that Jeffers had toured Europe in mid-1938, and had claimed he'd met with Mussolini and Hermann Goering. Sources also linked him to the pro-Nazi German-American Bund on the West Coast, and alleged that he would soon head up an anti-Semitic and anti-Catholic mass-movement in California.

Locally, Los Angeles DA Burton Fitts heard rumors that Jeffers planned to burn down the Kingdom Temple for insurance money, that he ran a smuggling ring, and that he and his new young wife Zella Joy were throwing "wild parties" at their Wilshire District high-rise flat. Fitts hired investigator Vincent Higgins to infiltrate the preacher's inner circle, and find out what dirty doings were happening therein.

The DA's office placed Higgins in an apartment adjacent to the couple's. Posing as a screenwriter interested in pitching Jeffers' life story to the studios, he introduced himself to the couple, and was invited over to their place for drinks one evening in March 1939. What happened that night got the Jeffers arrested for immoral conduct, and once again put the L.A. pastor in the national news.

During the sensational four-week trial that followed, Higgins testified that on the night he stopped by the Jeffers' flat, Zella Joy answered the door in sheer silk pajamas, with a welcoming glass of champagne in her hand. Sitting him down, she showed the investigator "French postcards"; when he expressed surprise at the novel sexual positions depicted on them, Zella sat in his lap and suggested that he needed a little instruction in the erotic arts. Zella and Joe then disrobed, Higgins said, and gave him a visual lesson in lovemaking. At that point he signaled police who were waiting in the hallway; they broke in with arrest warrants and cameras, and caught the nude, copulating couple on motion-picture film.

Another witness against the couple was Kingdom Temple member Marguerite Morgan. The attractive blonde beautician testified that one evening, when she accompanied Joe Jeffers to his flat for a nightcap, Zella had

Zella Jeffers takes the stand.

"I'm against Bolshevik Jews. They caused the Jews' downfall in Germany. I want to save my people from Communistic Jews."

answered the door stark naked. Like Higgins, Morgan was given bubbly, shown pornographic pictures, and treated to a live sex-show by the couple; papers of the time obliquely referred to an "unnatural act" they performed for her benefit.

Prosecutors played tape recordings and films that seemed to corroborate the testimony to the jury. They claimed that orgies were a regular occurrence at the Jeffers household, and that on one memorable evening, Zella Jeffers and a male lover copulated while the pair watched hubby Joe going at it with three women at once. In her sworn pre-trial testimony, Zella maintained she'd gone along with the sexual escapades because "I loved my husband and wanted to keep working with him to win him away from his peculiar ideas."

But on the witness stand, Zella denied everything. In tears, she claimed that their supposed "friend" Higgins had drugged the couple's champagne, and had "induced" the couple into immoral acts. At one point, the humiliated, hysterical woman ripped the court microphone off her sleeve and screamed, "Oh, it's unfair! I'm not getting a fair trial!"

When her husband took the stand, he claimed he'd been framed by "the Communist Jews," and named Jewish studio chiefs Harry and Jack Warner as the sting's instigators. During breaks in the proceedings, Jeffers rallied hundreds of his supporters in front of the courthouse, while countless other spectators tried to get into the courtroom for a gander at the lurid evidence and testimony.

The jury ultimately decided that the Jeffers had been entrapped, and found the couple not guilty. After the acquittal, Jeffers led his followers outside the courthouse in a sarcastic public mass-prayer for the Jews, as well as for the Catholics, the DA's office, and the rest of his supposed persecutors. When a reporter asked him if he was anti-Semitic, Jeffers responded, "I'm not against all Jews; we're really all Jews. But I 'm against Bolshevik Jews. They caused the Jews' downfall in Germany. I want to save my people from Communistic Jews. I 'm not a Jew-baiter. How could I be when I 'm a Jew myself?"

And as if to thumb his nose at Washington and the Warner Bros' suspicions about his Nazi sympathies, Jeffers soon afterwards hosted a recruiting night at Kingdom Temple for the L.A. branch of the Silver Legion, a Fascist paramilitary movement. Such antics didn't endear him to the authorities once the United States entered World War II; in 1943 the military interrogated Jeffers regarding his pro-Axis sentiments, and even considered banning him from the Fourth Army Corps territory as a dangerous subversive.

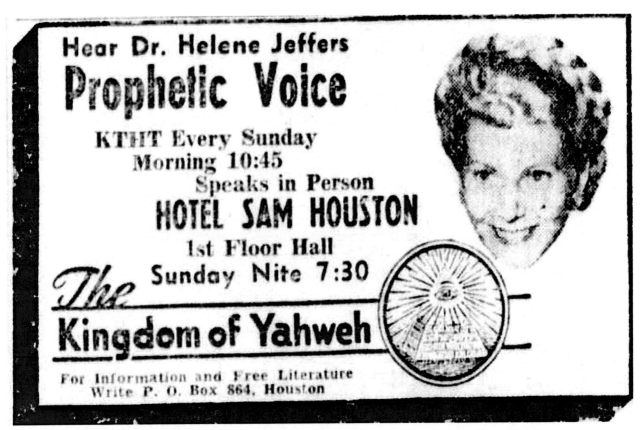

Helen Veborg, Jeffers' third wife, joined his ministry as a speaker and an author.

Limousines and Laurel Canyon

That year saw Jeffers in the courtroom and the headlines once again—this time, in a messy divorce case. Now claiming he was "Son of Yahweh, Ruler of the Universe", Jeffers said that Yahweh, from his home in the constellation Orion, had commanded him to father a "sacred child" in Florida with Helen Veborg, one of his many female followers and an aspiring actress.

Enraged, Zella Jeffers filed for a divorce. When the matter came to court, she alleged that Joe Jeffers was "under the delusion that he's Jesus reincarnated", and that Kingdom Temple, far from being a place of worship, was "a mere convenience through which he may and does do business for himself." The judge granted Zella her divorce, and awarded her alimony and a share of Jeffers' property, including "The Golden Chariot of Kingdom Come"—Jeffers' Cadillac limousine.

"We have been in communication with Yahweh for years. In the back of my head is a two-way radio set I use to talk to him."

Shortly after the ruling, Jeffers took Helene Veborg as his third wife. Then he commandeered the Caddy, and ordered his followers to "join with the chariot" on a convoy back to Florida. Arrested for driving the stolen vehicle across state lines, Jeffers was convicted for violating the Dyer Act, and served seventeen months in Federal prison.

When he was released on parole, he joined Helene in Florida, and soon returned to postwar Los Angeles, where most of his faithful followers resided. There he rented a 32-room mansion on Laurel Canyon Boulevard, and filled the house with middle-aged women whom he charged up to $100,000 to share living quarters with the Son of Yahweh and his wife. Jeffers also predicted that a nuclear war would hit L.A. in 1949, and bought an 823-acre survival retreat near Palm Springs that he dubbed "Yahweh Springs."

Soon, Jeffers was back in court. When he led his Laurel Canyon followers in a noisy, predawn, outdoor prayer to Yahweh for money, he was busted for disturbing the peace, charged with a zoning violation, and fined. Weeks later, more than a dozen disciples sued him for fraud and misrepresentation, claiming that Jeffers had pocketed their donations and stiffed them on various contracts. The Son of Yahweh had to settle more than $50,000 worth of claims, and the bad publicity slowed the flow of "love offerings" into the Kingdom's coffers.

Finally, Zella Jeffers took her estranged husband to court for nonpayment of alimony. Facing the judge, Jeffers claimed that although Yahweh had given him $5 billion for his services, the cash was located in the constellation Orion, and therefore inaccessible for payment of his Earthly debts. In the meantime, Jeffers said, he was worth exactly $1.53 American, and turned out his pockets for the judge's benefit.

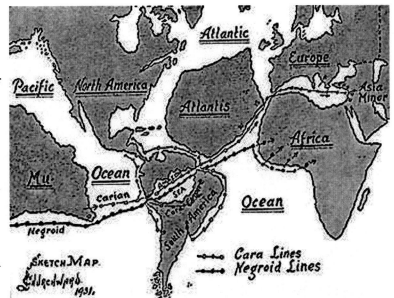

James Churchward

The lost continents of Atlantis and Mu (Lemuria).

When the judge asked Jeffers how he could afford to maintain a car he kept, the prophet responded: "Yahweh has all the automobiles in the world. He can use them any time he wants… We have been in communication with Yahweh for years. In the back of my head is a two-way radio set I use to talk to him. It's two-way, you see, 'Yah' going out to Orion and 'Weh' coming back to me."

Jeffers also boasted to the court of his necromantic dealings with a dead demagogue. "We know everything President Truman does" he told them, "because Huey Long covers the White House for us." Unimpressed, the judge ruled for Zella, and the Son of Yahweh was sent back to the Federal pen for parole violation.

Atlantis, Reincarnation, and Murder

When he was finally released, Jeffers moved to Phoenix, Arizona. Billing himself as "Dr. Joseph Jeffers," he and Helene spread the Yahwist message during the 1950s via the lecture circuit and self-published books and pamphlets.

Jeffers' Yahwist doctrine soon sported distinctly occult flavorings. He maintained that Atlantis and Lemuria were real places that had drowned in a prehistoric flood when their peoples turned their back on Yahweh, but would rise again from the Atlantic and the Pacific, and usher in a New Age of Mankind where multiple Suns would light the Earth and banish darkness and baleful moonlight forever. He also advocated a vegetarian, raw-food diet for his followers, and performed "reincarnation revelations" for them, tapping into the Akashic records and viewing their previous incarnations.

By the mid-1950s, Jeffers had divorced Helen, and took her eighteen year-old secretary, Connie Bernice, as his fourth wife. Helene set up herself up as a psychic-phenomena lecturer in Denver, Colorado, where in February 1957, she was attacked, raped, and murdered in her office by an assailant. The murder has never been solved.

Eight years later, Joseph and Connie Jeffers were arrested after an investigation revealed that the couple had been betting church funds on dog and horse races in Phoenix. The Jeffers claimed that "games of chance were a part of the congregation's metaphysical research and study of extrasensory perception," but the judge didn't buy it, and convicted them on thirteen counts of mail fraud. But in 1968 the Ninth Circuit Court reversed the conviction, stating that "The spectacle presented to the jury—of a 67 year old eccentric purporting to have psychic powers, and his attractive 27 year old wife betting contributors' funds at the dog races—was so highly prejudicial that we cannot conclude that a fair trial was had…."

By the 1970s, the Jeffers had relocated to Missouri, not too far from where Jeffers had fought the Jonesboro Church Wars forty years earlier. They bought a 350-acre tract near the town of St. James, and set up a communal center to house themselves and a few dozen followers. The centerpiece of the community was the "Temple"—a pyramid-shaped, 28-foot tall tabernacle that Jeffers said would serve as a refuge from a nuclear attack, as well as a beacon for Yahweh's spaceships when they arrived from Orion during the Apocalypse.

Legacy Battles and Death

If Jeffers had any plans to spend his late 70s peacefully awaiting the Second Coming, they were quickly dashed. First, Connie divorced him. Then they remarried. Then she left him again, this time taking with her several million dollars the couple had stashed in the Kingdom bank account. When Jeffers pursued his estranged wife to Florida in 1978, he and two of his lieutenants were arrested, and charged with conspiring to murder her. The authorities also charged the 79 year-old prophet with statutory rape of a 14 year-old girl at the Kingdom compound.

Yahweh's New Kingdom publishes Jeffers' writings on lost continents—among many other subjects.

LEMURIA

ATLANTIS

HISTORY REWRITTEN

BY DR. JOSEPH JEFFERS
& THE KINGDOM STAFF

Luckily for Jeffers, authorities eventually dropped all the charges. He also won a court judgment against his wife over the pilfered millions, and finalized a second divorce with her in 1979.

That year, he once again relocated the Kingdom of Yahweh—this time, to Texas. There he fought a long court battle over the legacy of one of his elderly followers, who had changed her will to make Jeffers the sole beneficiary of her $5 million estate, then died shortly afterwards under mysterious circumstances. Jeffers eventually settled with the woman's heirs for about $150,000 and some real estate.

In his eighties, Jeffers returned to Arizona, and remained active, researching and writing profusely. He kept abreast of revisionist history and theology, adapting ideas by controversial Biblical scholars like John Allegro and Michael Baigent, as well as the latest translations and theories regarding the Dead Sea Scrolls and other apocryphal works.

Finally, on July 11, 1988, the 89 year-old Prophet left his aged body and joined Yahweh in Orion for eternity. The Kingdom was taken over by longtime Jeffers associate Philip Evans—a position he holds to this day.

Jeffers' church, now called *Yahweh's New Kingdom*, exists today mainly as a Web site and a monthly newsletter. The Kingdom produces hundreds of booklets and pamphlets by Jeffers and others, with titles like "Scriptural Proofs of Reincarnation," "Onward Christian Cannibals," and "What Yahweh Thinks of Christmas."

The Son of Yahweh may not have lived to see his beloved Father bring forth the New World that he'd prophesied since his days as a 20-something Fundamentalist Baptist preacher. But he did leave a unique legacy to the spiritual landscape of both California and the United States as a whole—a fringe-Adventist spirituality colored with esoteric and occult elements, and a scandal-plagued life and career with few parallels anywhere in the modern Christian world.

7

Herbert W. Armstrong & the Worldwide Church of God

While Joe Jeffers and the Kingdom of Yahweh never gained more than a modest following, Pasadena's Herbert W. Armstrong and his Worldwide Church of God became a global movement with a six-figure flock, radio and TV audiences numbering in the millions, and probably the most visible and influential of fringe-Adventist Christian sects during its heyday.

Adventism, Anti-Trinitarianism, and British Israel

Born in 1892, Armstrong was an Iowa native who settled in Oregon in 1924, and accepted Jesus Christ as his Savior three years later. Although a nominal Baptist, Armstrong felt the denomination was unfaithful to the whole of Biblical teachings, and left it in 1928 to join the Church of God (Seventh Day), the oldest and most traditional of the Adventist churches.

Herbert W. Armstrong

Adventism grew out of the teachings of William Miller, who in 1844 convinced over 50,000 followers that Jesus Christ would return to Earth and usher in the Millennium, in an episode now viewed as a classic example of mass religious hysteria. When the Messiah failed to arrive on the various days Miller had scheduled his return, the movement split into several competing factions, the largest of which became Ellen G. White's Seventh-Day Adventist Church.

Seventh-Day Adventists believed that Saturday was the truth Seventh Day of Sabbath mandated by Scripture. They observed Old Testament dietary laws and spurned pork, shellfish, and other "unclean meats" in their diets. They rejected Christmas, Easter, and other traditional Christian holidays, seeing them as pagan feasts grafted onto the Church. And their churches financed themselves through members' tithing, and emphasized Biblical prophecy and the role of the United States as a modern extension of Israel.

Armstrong became a Seventh-Day Adventist minister in 1931, but soon got in a bitter dispute within the church over leadership and doctrine. Siding with the minority faction, who advocated non-democratic church government and the strict observance of Jewish feast days, Armstrong broke with the church's main body to affiliate with the dissident group based out of Salem, West Virginia.

By this time, Armstrong had set up the two media outlets that would become his mouthpieces for the next fifty years. On radio station KORE

The Plain Truth's first issue, February 1934

An 1885 map illustrates the British-Israelite theory that the "Lost Tribe of Dan" crossed ancient Europe and settled in the British Isles.

in Eugene, he began broadcasting *The Radio Church of God*, dispensing Adventist doctrine over the 100-watt transmitter's range. To supplement the broadcasts, he published a mimeographed newsletter called *The Plain Truth*, and distributed it to his listeners.

Armstrong's own theology contained two key elements that carried his ministry far from orthodox Christianity, and even from the Adventist Church of God. One of them was his denial of the Trinity, which he said was a false, quasi-Pagan concept that had perverted Christian teachings. Armstrong preached that God was instead a "family," consisting of the Father, His Son Jesus, and all other saved Christians. As for the Holy Spirit, It was not a "person," but the action of God, shared by the Father and the Son.

British-Israelism taught that the Ten Lost Tribes of Israel settled in the British Isles, and that modern British and Anglo-Americans were their genetic and spiritual descendants.

To the non-Trinitarian theology, Armstrong added an even more unorthodox teaching: the doctrine of British-Israelism. Also known as Anglo-Israelism, the doctrine maintained that Anglo-American Christians were the literal, lineal blood descendants of ancient Israel and thereby genetically and spiritually mandated to observe Saturday Sabbath, the Jewish festivals, and Old Testament dietary restrictions.

Originating in early Victorian England, British-Israelism taught that the Lost Ten Tribes of Israel had escaped Babylonian captivity, migrated to Europe, and settled in the British Isles—the land of the *Beyrith iysh*, or, "people of the Covenant." The tribes' migrations were recorded in European place-names; the Danube, Don, and Dniester Rivers, for example, were named after the Tribe of Dan, as was the Irish *Tuatha de Danaan*. The British Royal Family, from James I to Elizabeth II, was a continuation of Davidian royalty, with their Coronation Stone being the very same rock that Jacob used as a pillow in *Genesis 28:18*. And the sub-tribes of Ephraim and Manasseh were the people of modern Britain and the United States; any Biblical prophecies mentioning these two groups actually referred to events in the present-day nations.

Rejected by mainstream Biblical and historical scholars, British Israelism persists to this day as a belief in certain fringe-Adventist sects. The Church of God (Seventh Day) saw Armstrong's teaching of it, as well as his anti-Trinitarian theology, heretical, and asked him to leave their fold in 1937. But by then, Armstrong had already established a sizable independent following via his radio program and newsletter, and founded his own sect: the Radio Church of God.

A Worldwide Church

During the 1940s, Armstrong expanded the Radio Church of God's ministry to six different stations, and turned *The Plain Truth* into a slick printed journal, distributed in the thousands. He also took his crusade from the airwaves to the streets, interviewing, baptizing, and receiving his radio listeners into his Church, which was fast becoming a true body of worship rather than a media ministry. Soon he was ordaining ministers as well.

Armstrong relocated to Pasadena, California, in 1946, and opened Ambassador College there as a seminary and Church headquarters. Seven years later his radio show, *The World Tomorrow*, debuted on Radio Luxembourg, the world's most powerful commercial station, and brought him millions of British and European listeners, as well as thousands of new Church members.

The Armstrongs urged believers not to vote, serve in the military, use cosmetics, marry after divorce, go to doctors, or celebrate "pagan" holidays like Christmas.

In 1957, Armstrong's son, Garner Ted Armstrong, joined his ministry. A charismatic figure with movie-star looks and a golden voice, the younger Armstrong increasingly became the public face of the Church, whose broadcasts now warned listeners that various natural disasters, wars, diseases, and social upheavals were "Signs of the Times" that hearkened Christ's return. To prepare for His coming, the Armstrongs urged believers not to vote, serve in the military, use cosmetics, marry after divorce, go to doctors, celebrate "pagan" holidays like Christmas, or otherwise conform to the dictates of a broken and sinful world.

The Church saw the *Book of Revelation* as a prophecy of the history and fate of Christendom through seven periods, as symbolized by the Seven Churches of chapters 2 and 3. Armstrong Sr. also taught that major Church events happened in 19-year cycles; he cited the beginning of his radio and magazine ministry in 1934, followed by the debut of international broadcasts on Radio Luxembourg in 1953, as one of these periods. Many

Garner Ted Armstrong.

Church faithful believed that the next 19-year marker, 1972, was the target date for Apocalypse, and watched the tumultuous events of the Sixties unfold with an air of fervent expectation.

In 1968, the church was renamed The Worldwide Church of God. To live up to the new title, Armstrong Senior purchased a private jet and traveled across the earth to meet and have his picture taken with various national presidents, premiers, monarchs, and dictators. The heads of state who posed with the septuagenarian, gnome-like Armstrong often had no idea who he was; they'd usually been primed beforehand with gifts and charitable donations by Armstrong's advance men, and were happy to accept Church largesse in exchange for a photo or meeting. Garner Ted later claimed that the Church spent up to $1 million a year greasing dignitaries for these photo-op sessions, which he privately dismissed as "the world's most expensive autograph hunt."

These photos regularly appeared in *The Plain Truth,* now a glossy color magazine that circulated as many as nine million free copies per issue. Along with the elder Armstrong's doings, it featured exposition of Church doctrines, as well as shots and stories of the Church's $50 million Ambassador University in Pasadena, which provided students with both a Christian liberal education and training for WWCG ministry.

And Garner Ted expanded his own ministry onto television, hosting a video version of *The World Tomorrow.* During the 1960s the junior Armstrong was one of the most visible of the television evangelists, viewed by millions across the globe.

Controversy, Scandal, and 60 Minutes

The high visibility of the Church disturbed more orthodox Christians, who felt that the Armstrongs' idiosyncratic doctrines distorted the Christian Gospel, and led believers into error, if not outright heresy. Especially disturbing to critics was the British-Israelite teaching, which many saw as a racist, exclusionary dogma that misrepresented Judeo-Christian history and spirituality, and undercut Christian efforts to reach out to the Third World. Too, many felt that the WWCG's mandatory 20-30% tithe on members was excessive; a good number of Church faithful struggled in poverty, they maintained, while the Armstrongs collected their tithes and lived in jet-set luxury.

By the 1970s, serious problems were afoot in the Worldwide Church of God. When 1972 came and passed without the slightest hint of Apocalypse, many WWCG faithful who had prepared for Jesus' return that year were angry at the elder Armstrong, even though he claimed he'd never set a date for the Day of Reckoning. There were also fierce internal disputes over Church doctrine. And when Herbert Armstrong married a divorcee nearly 50 years younger than himself, many WWCG members—chief among them Garner Ted—felt it was an open violation of Church strictures against remarriage. During this time, several ministers and their followers left the WWCG and formed splinter groups based on the original teachings, but independent of the Armstrongs and their hierarchical Church authority.

Garner Ted's own behavior created even more consternation than his father's did. In 1972, he confessed to his father that he had had affairs with more than 200 Ambassador College undergraduates, Church ministers' wives, and other women over a 20-year period. Although rumors about Garner Ted's sexual activities had been rampant in the Church for many years, the private but widely-publicized confession, and pressure from Church insiders, forced the elder Armstrong to excommunicate his son, and remove him from his various WWCG posts, including hosting *The World Tomorrow* and leading Ambassador College.

Garner Ted claimed that his father had sexually molested his younger sister throughout the 1930s and 1940s.

But several months later, Armstrong Sr. allowed his son back into the fold. Herbert would expel Garner Ted three more times in the 1970s, yet always invite and welcome the Prodigal Son back into the Church, even though the younger Armstrong continued to scandalize the WWCG with more extramarital affairs, and a bad gambling habit financed by Church funds. Whatever his failings, Garner Ted was a gifted preacher and an international celebrity whose absence from the scene cost the WWCG dearly; one report said that Church revenue dropped as much as 40 percent when the younger Armstrong wasn't working TV audiences for donations.

When he was in favor with his father, Garner Ted effectively ran the entire WWCG organization during Herbert's extended trips across the globe. Still, he constantly quarreled with Armstrong Sr. about management and doctrinal interpretations, and believed that Church hierarchs were manipulating his elderly and forgetful father against him. The final break came in 1978, when Herbert permanently expelled Garner Ted from the Church, and the younger Armstrong went off to form his own Church of God, International, based out of Tyler, Texas.

On April 15, 1979, the weekly television news show *60 Minutes* broadcast a segment that examined the charges brought against the Church by then-California Attorney General George Deukmejian, on behalf of Garner Ted and other dissident WWCG members. The investigation focused on Stanley Rader, an accountant and convert from Judaism who had become one of the senior Armstrong's closest advisors, and who was accused of massively misappropriating Church funds, cutting insider deals, laundering money, and similar dirty doings. The segment's most telling moment was during an interview with Rader, when journalist Mike Wallace played him a tape of Herbert Armstrong surmising that the accountant was plotting to take over the organization after his death.

Rader spent millions in Church funds to block attempted audits and litigation against the WWCG, which had been placed in temporary receivership by the state. He fought the Attorney General's office all the way to the Supreme Court, and relentlessly lobbied the state legislature to protect the Church, himself, and Armstrong Senior against the investigation. The latter effort resulted in the passage of the *Petris* law, which greatly restricted the ability of the State Attorney General to investigate religious groups. Eventually Rader left the Church amicably, with a reported six-figure "golden handshake" for his efforts in saving it from legal extinction.

Between 1989 and 2005, the Church lost up to two-thirds of its membership.

On January 16, 1986, the 93-year-old Herbert Armstrong passed away, under the shadow of an ugly sex scandal of his own. Several years earlier, Garner Ted had told WWCG critic David Robinson that his father had sexually molested his younger sister Dorothy throughout the 1930s and 1940s. When Robinson interviewed Herbert and Dorothy, they admitted to the incestuous relationship, and it became a point of contention during the senior Armstrong's 1984 divorce from his second wife.

Schism, Reform, and Reinvention

With both Garner Ted and Stanley Rader gone, Church leadership fell to Herbert W. Armstrong's appointed successor, Joseph W. Tkach. Tkach inherited a small ecclesiastical empire with between 120,000 and 140,000 members scattered across the globe, an estimated income of $170 million a year, large property holdings that included the flagship Ambassador College in Pasadena, and the legacy of scandal left by the founder and his associates.

Once he took the helm, Tkach instituted gradual but overwhelming changes in the Church's doctrines that virtually erased the innovations that had made the WWCG distinct among Christian denominations. During his tenure, the WWCG lifted the prohibitions against cosmetics, divorce, and other "worldly" practices. It also took a huge step towards mainstream Christian theology in 1994 when it adapted the orthodox Trinitarian formulation as an official doctrine. Tithing was made optional, as was the Saturday Sabbath, and celebrations of Jewish festivals. And most devastating of all, British-Israelism—the core prophetic doctrine of the Church since its inception—was declared to be historically and hermeneutically inaccurate, and purged from official teachings.

Many observers felt that the real figure driving the doctrinal changes was Tkach's son, Joe Junior. Educated at the non-denominational Christian Azusa Pacific University, Joe

Jr. had begun to question WWCG beliefs, and eventually not only rejected most of the Church's characteristic doctrines, but also influenced his father to do the same. When the senior Tkach began to suffer from ill health, his son took over the reins of Church administration, with his father standing in as a figurehead. Since Tkach Senior had been Herbert Armstrong's handpicked successor, Church faithful, used to the top-down hierarchical administration, initially went along with the first changes.

An account of the WWCG's transformation.

But the Tkaches underestimated the loyalty of the Armstrongs' followers. Many of them had spent their entire lives inside the Church, and had embraced Herbert Armstrong's vision of a British-Israelite, non-Trinitarian, Old-Testament Christianity as the road to Salvation. They had forgiven Armstrong Senior and Junior their indiscretions, and had looked the other way while Stanley Rader finagled Church funds, so long as those leaders had stayed true to the original doctrines. When those doctrines were excised from the church, tens of thousands of faithful followed in a mass exodus.

It's estimated that up to two-thirds of the WCG membership—as many as 100,000 people —left between 1989 and 2005, in a schism with few precedents in American religious history. Many of the members followed dissident Church ministers into splinter groups like the United Church of God, the Philadelphia Church of God, and the Living Church of God. There are believed to be over 200 of these schismatic churches today, as well as hundreds of informal "house churches", that stay faithful to the original Armstrongian teachings to one degree or another.

Few Church traditionalists, however, sided with the most famous and visible World-wide Church of God dissident: Garner Ted Armstrong. In 1995 he was thrown out of his own Church of God, International, after Geraldo Rivera's tabloid TV show broadcast a tape of the 65 year-old evangelist making sexual advances to a masseuse. Three years later, Garner Ted formed the Intercontinental Church of God, but it attracted few followers. He died in 2003 of complications from pneumonia.

Today the Worldwide Church of God is now known as Grace Communion International, based in Glendora, California, and claims a mere 50,000 members, down from an estimated 140,000 at the time of Armstrong Senior's death. Ambassador College, along with many other Church properties and assets, was sold, and *The Plain Truth* ceased publication in 1986. The Church's current doctrines are almost indistinguishable from any other Evangelical Protestant Church; many Christian commentators, although pleased by the group's return to relative orthodoxy, have questioned why it even exists as a distinct organization today. As for the splinter groups, scores of them continue to function, each one claiming heirship to the true Armstrongian doctrine.

The Church itself, acknowledging its painful transition from heterodox sect to mainstream evangelical group, says, "Jesus is not done with us yet. We are still being shaped and fashioned for his purpose." What that purpose is for the church, or for the many schismatic Armstrongite groups, remains to be seen.

8

Dr. Gene Scott & the Faith Center Church

It seems inconceivable that the city of Pasadena, famed for its old-money conservatism and quiet elegance, could have been the home of not one but *two* deeply-unorthodox, hugely-controversial, multi-millionaire television-evangelists. Yet for many years, the town that gave the world Caltech and the Rose Parade was headquarters for not only Herbert W. Armstrong, but the phenomenon known as Dr. Gene Scott.

If Herbert W. Armstrong was the Paul Harvey of heterodox Christianity, Dr. Gene Scott was its Howard Stern. For nearly 30 years, Scott presided over a one-man television ministry that had no parallel even in the colorful world of televangelism. Combining the showmanship of Aimee Semple McPherson, the theological idiosyncrasies of Joe Jeffers, the flamboyance of King Louis Narcisse, and the sheer greed of C. Thomas Patten, Scott joked, pleaded, blustered, bullied, and threatened his way into a worldwide TV audience, a sizeable fortune, and a singular role as the outlaw and wild man of the video preachers.

Jack Boulware

Dr Gene Scott lampooned by the satirical magazine, THE NOSE

"Get on the Phone!"

Like those of his predecessors, Scott's origins were relatively mundane. Born on August 14, 1929, he was the son of a traveling preacher and his teenaged wife. Raised in his father's Assembly of God church in Gridley, California, he was from an early age an exceptional student and voracious reader. Scott's academic talents eventually brought him to Stanford University, where he earned a Doctorate of Educational Philosophy in 1957.

After leaving Stanford, Scott taught in a Midwestern Bible college, and helped Oral Roberts establish his university in Tulsa, Oklahoma. Taking a cue from his father, Scott became a traveling preacher for the Assemblies of God, and quickly established a reputation as a gifted evangelist and thinker. Scott split amicably with the denomination in 1970, and joined his father in Oroville, California to establish an independent ministry.

While he was conducting this mission, the younger Scott was contacted by the Faith Center Church, and offered leadership of the organization. A long-established evangelical ministry located downstate in Glendale, the Church was $3.5 million in debt, and needed a fresh, dynamic leader to attract new blood to the congregation. Scott agreed to head the Church so long as the current leaders stepped out of the way, and gave him near-total control over the organization and its four independently-owned TV stations. The desperate leaders agreed to the terms, and in 1975 Scott took the helm of the Faith Center Church.

"Kill a Pissant for Jesus!"

Scott took full advantage of the Church's four broadcast stations, and started an evangelical TV program called *Festival of Faith* that was soon bringing in much-needed money and followers. Within a decade, the small network was carrying Scott's sermons and fund-raising programs 24 hours a day, seven days a week, on a signal that reached most of North America and the Caribbean.

In the beginning, Scott conformed to the standard image of a televangelist. Neatly coiffed and dressed in a three-piece suit, Dr. Gene presented viewers with a fairly standard brand of Evangelical Christian doctrine, interspersed with pleas for donations.

"A skinflint may get to Heaven, but what awaits him are a rusty old halo, a skinny old cloud, and a robe so worn it scratches. First-class salvation costs money."

But by the late 1970s, Scott was pioneering new, strange territory not explored by any TV preacher before or since. He grew his hair long, sprouted a bushy beard, and swapped conservative suits for jeans and cowboy hats. His sermons became rambling, profanity-laden diatribes on subjects ranging from current events, to the follies of mainstream religion, to the enormities of his ex-wife, whom he called "the Devil's sister." His studio band played Dr. Scott originals like "Kill a Pissant for Jesus" along with gospel standards. And unlike the silver-tongued seducers of donation-driven televangelism, Scott crudely bullied and browbeat his viewers for love offerings; his command, "Get on the phone!" became a catchphrase of the ministry.

First Fruits and the FCC

Dr. Scott vaulted into national notoriety in the early 1980s, when the Federal Communications Commission launched an investigation of Faith Center Church's mini-network, after former employees accused Scott of diverting Church funds into his private coffers. Scott refused to cooperate with the investigation, and although the charges were never proven, the Church ended up losing ownership of three of its four stations. The California Attorney General also tried to investigate Scott for fraud, but was stymied by the passage of the Worldwide Church of God-sponsored *Petris* bill, which hamstrung State probes of religious groups.

Seeking to reclaim and expand his electronic ministry, Scott used Church funds to buy up airtime on any local station or cable-TV outlet that would take his money. He also beamed his shows to a nationwide audience via satellite, and broadcast them on medium- and shortwave-radio to the world in four languages. By 1990, *Festival of Faith* reached 180 different countries, saturating worldwide airwaves.

Viewers who happened to channel-surf onto a Dr. Gene Scott show encountered a television ministry unlike any other. His bearded, long-haired countenance wreathed in a cloud of cigar smoke, and topped with a cowboy hat, fedora, sombrero, or other distinctive head-gear, Scott stared down the camera with a piercing, steely glare. And his sermons, when he deigned to discuss things spiritual, taught his own quirky brand of Christianity.

Scott's theology was an eclectic mélange of doctrines. He promoted British-Israelism as well as pyramidology, an occult teaching that believes secrets and prophecies are hidden in the Great Pyramid of Giza's dimensions. Too, Scott defended Creationism, the physical Resurrection, and other fundamentalist beliefs with the skill of an erudite academic, scribbling complex notes and diagrams onto a whiteboard to illustrate a point or concept.

And he solicited donations… shamelessly. Although thousands of Scott's followers were alleged to contribute a hefty $350 a month per person to the ministry, there was never enough income to satisfy the cigar-chomping televangelist. Scott demanded, along with a 10% weekly tithe of income, a mandatory contribution of his followers' "first fruits"—the first return on any sort of income, including investments, tax refunds, second jobs, or even gambling winnings or unemployment benefits.

He'd also stage regular appeals for funds to finance enigmatic projects or fend off unspecified threats. For one of these fundraisers, "Secret V," Scott ordered 700 followers to send at least $10,000 apiece, and 3,000 more to pony up a minimum of $1,000 each, so that he could raise $10 million for some project so vital to the Church that he couldn't describe it on the air. From solicitations like this, as well as from tithing, first fruits and other sources, Scott was estimated to pull in an average take of over $1 million a month.

And woe unto the Gene Scott follower that refused to cough up the funds! "A skinflint may get to Heaven," the Doctor warned deadbeats, "but what awaits him are

Werner Herzog's documentary film about Scott. Its English title was "God's Angry Man."

a rusty old halo, a skinny old cloud, and a robe so worn it scratches. First-class salvation costs money." Scott maintained that holding out on him was tantamount to cheating the Almighty Himself, and "if you get too smart with God, he might let you live this next year without him so you can see the difference."

Down the Slimy Chute Straight to Hell

Dr. Scott's naked avarice, eccentric demeanor, and bizarre sermonizing attracted a cult following among TV viewers who normally would've tuned out televangelists. Celebrities like Johnny Carson, Burt Reynolds, and Paul Newman were reputed to be Dr. Gene fans, holding private TV parties where they'd laugh at the preacher's antics and crank-call the Church's 800 number. Robin Williams lampooned Dr. Scott on a *Saturday Night Live* episode, and German film director Werner Herzog was so fascinated by the pastor's ability to raise several hundred thousand dollars in a few minutes that he made a documentary about him called *God's Angry Man.*

> *"I don't ask you to change when you come here. I take you as you are, as God takes me as I am."*

Everyone had a different "favorite" episode of *Festival of Faith.* For some, it was the time when Dr. Scott was fighting the FCC, and he broadcast from a roomful of chattering, wind-up toy monkeys that he likened to the Feds, and then smashed to pieces with a baseball bat. Another choice segment was when, dissatisfied with the level of donations coming in from viewers, Scott sat in his chair and glared into the camera for a full ten minutes without batting an eyelash or uttering a word. Often, the screen would split and a second Dr. Scott would pop up and start a running commentary about the *doppelganger's* taped sermon. And of course, he would relentlessly, continuously bait and badger his camera crew, his volunteer phone staff, and both his live and TV audiences, whom he promised would slide "down the slimy chute straight to Hell" if they didn't kick in enough dough to meet his fund-raising goals.

Part of what appealed to Dr. Scott's fans was that he never pushed the judgmental, legalistic side of Evangelical Christianity. "I don't ask you to change when you come here," he would tell his viewers. "I take you as you are, as God takes me as I am." Scott refused to condemn homosexuality, adultery, profanity, abortion, or drinking, and even shied away from the title of televangelist: "In every way possible within the boundaries of God's word," he said, "I have tried to separate from the television evangelists' image. Television evangelism has become a phrase that can only become analogized to nigger, kike, beaner and other epithets designed to demean and create a perceptual set of a lesser-quality being."

And for all of his brazen donation-grubbing, Dr. Scott did generously support charities and good works. During his career, he raised $2 million to repair and restock the Los Angeles Library after a fire, and spent $430,000 to help a Pasadena public swim center. Scott subsidized various city and state projects as well, earning kudos from political movers like L.A. City Council member Joel Wachs and California Assembly leader Willie Brown. And he spent over $2 million to renovate the historic United Artists Theatre at Broadway and Olympic, turning it into the worship center for his Los Angeles University Cathedral and revitalizing the depressed neighborhood around the building.

Still, Dr. Scott wasn't one to pursue the lifestyle of an impoverished mendicant. The countless millions his followers and volunteers raised helped him live as lavishly as any of the first-magnitude televangelists of the 1980s. Scott lived in a Pasadena mansion filled with rare art, stamps, coins, books, and other collectibles. He became a top breeder of show horses, and kept over 100 of them stabled on two multimillion-dollar ranches in Southern California and Kentucky.

Pastor or Porn Star?

True to Scott's scandalous form, *Festival of Faith* often showed footage of bikini-clad models riding his thoroughbreds, with the preacher gloating to his audience about "what I got waitin' for me at home." One of the models, Melissa Pastore, was a special favorite of Scott's—so much so, that in 1998 he ordained her as an administrative pastor, even though she had no ministerial education or training. Two years later, the 70 year-old televangelist and the 32 year-old junior pastor wed in Reno.

One month after the wedding, Scott was diagnosed with prostate cancer. Spurning surgery and chemotherapy, he continued to sermonize and broadcast for the next four years as the cancer metastasized through his body. Eventually he was hospitalized, and on February 21, 2005, a massive stroke felled the 75 year-old maverick.

Both Scott's lavish estate and his television ministry passed to wife Melissa. A self-taught scholar who claimed to speak 25 languages, Melissa Scott took the helm of *Festival of Faith* with aplomb, and faithfully taught her late husband's doctrines, even scrawling on a whiteboard for the TV cameras much as he had. But she eschewed his on-camera rants and shenanigans, and focused on no-nonsense Biblical exegetics. She also traveled to and from University Cathedral with a squad of bodyguards, and lived away from Scott's $17 million Pasadena mansion. Some observers speculated she was hiding from something.

Those speculations heated up when church members began to receive anonymous letters and emails with photos of porn star "Barbie Bridges" in various explicit nude poses. Ms. Bridges bore a striking resemblance to *Festival of Faith*'s new hostess, and both Gene Scott Web groups and the Scotts' Wikipedia pages were deluged with postings of more of her photos, and assertions that she and Pastor Melissa were the same person. Although Melissa Scott vehemently denied the rumors, and threatened legal actions against church members who spread them, a 2009 article by Gretchen Voss in *Marie Claire* magazine featured statements from several of her close acquaintances, as well as her ex-husband Paul Pastore, that confirmed the lady televangelist was in fact the ex-porn-star and nude-model, who abandoned that career when she met Dr. Gene.

Pastor Melissa Scott is alleged to be former porn-star Barbie Bridges.

To this day Scott denies she was Barbie Bridges—a stance that has disappointed some of the faithful, who see in the porn-star-turned-pastor tale a living illustration of the transformative power Christ can bring to sinners. She continues to broadcast talks and sermons on local TV stations, cable channels, and the Internet, and holds live Sunday

Pastor Melissa Scott, formerly known as porn star "Barbie Bridges"

services at the Faith Center in Glendale, where Gene Scott began his ministry over forty years ago.

And Pastor Melissa makes sure Gene Scott lives on, in the form of the countless thousands of hours of *Festival of Faith* videotapes continually rerun on TV, satellite, shortwave radio, and streaming Web broadcasts. Through the miracles of magnetic media and data transmissions, California's—and possibly America's—most outrageous and unabashed televangelist should be berating, bewildering, and bedazzling multimedia audiences for a long time to come.

9
Wesley Swift
& Christian Identity

Whe Gene Scott or the Armstrongs were asked about British Israelism's implications for non-Anglo-Saxon peoples, they always stressed that they weren't racists or anti-Semites. God loved all His children, they insisted, and if anything, having an ancient-Israelite bloodline made White Christians *more* obligated to behave gently and righteously towards people of color and modern-day Jews.

No such disclaimers troubled the career of Reverend Wesley Albert Swift, late of Lancaster, California. The founder of the Church of Jesus Christ—Christian, Swift spent four decades transforming British Israelism from an eccentric Biblical-revisionist doctrine, into a racist ideology that portrayed non-Whites as sub-humans and Jews as Satanic schemers, and inspired terrorism that has claimed lives across the United States.

Wesley and wife, Olive Lorraine.

Tribes of Israel, Sons of Cain

A New Jersey native, Swift was licensed at 18 as a preacher in the segregationist Methodist Episcopal Church, South. Soon afterwards he migrated to Los Angeles, where he studied at Philip E.J. Monson's Kingdom Bible College, which taught the doctrines of Howard Rand, a British Israelite and the founder of the Anglo-Saxon Federation of America.

While other Californian British Israelites maintained that modern-day Jewish people—"the tribe of Judah"—were related to Saxons and Celts via the "Lost Tribes of Israel", Rand and his followers claimed that 20th Century Jews were Canaanites—descendants of Isaac's son Esau, who had lost his birthright to his brother Jacob, and had married outside

Harris & Ewing.

Far-Right firebrand, Gerald L.K. Smith

the Abrahamic lineage. To them, today's so-called "Jews" were impostors, whereas the true Israelites had been dispersed into Northern and Western Europe, and became the White race of today.

Married to this doctrine was an even more sinister concept. Randian British Israelites taught that Adam and Eve were the first true humans, created by God in about 7400 BC to have dominion over "the beasts of the field"—the prototype pseudo-humans who were identified with the non-White races. The fall from Eden came, they said, when Eve mated with the Serpent and birthed Cain, who then murdered his half-brother Abel, married into the Hittite beast-tribe, and formed the Canaanite nation that Esau later joined.

In this doctrine, Jews were literally demonic — a serpentine, pseudo-human pestilence that had lied and tricked the White race into economic and political servitude, and spiritual and racial alienation. And White Gentiles were the lost children of Israel—the Chosen People of God, and the natural masters of the planet.

Swift absorbed and embraced this theology during the 1930s, and spent the rest of the decade preaching the Gospel of Randian British-Israelism to any audience that would listen. His best gig of the era was at Aimee Semple MacPherson's Foursquare Temple, where he served as a warm-up act for the fading Pentecostal superstar.

Christian Knights of the Invisible Empire

By the 1940s America was fighting a total war against another Jew-bashing, master-race ideology, and Swift's sermons generally fell on deaf or hostile ears. But the Southern Californian pastor attracted one key convert to his cause: the legendary preacher and rabble-rouser Gerald L.K. Smith.

Originally a Disciples of Christ minister, Smith was a charismatic speaker and demagogue whom iconoclastic journalist H.L. Mencken called "the greatest orator of them all, not the greatest by an inch or a foot or a yard or a mile, but the greatest by at least two light years." Openly racist and anti-Semitic, the self-declared "Christian Nationalist" Smith was America's most visible far-Right leader into the 1940's, and was tried—unsuccessfully—for sedition by the US government during World War II.

Smith met Wesley Swift in 1947, three years after the sedition trial. Impressed by the 34 year-old preacher, whom he called an "eloquent and crusading clergyman," Smith made Swift his West Coast representative, and shared the pulpit with him at his California appearances, including a Hollywood rally that they claimed was picketed by "nearly 20,000 Reds and their Dupes." Their talks merged nascent Cold War paranoia with "Biblically-based" anti-Semitic and White-Supremacist rhetoric, asserting that America was under siege from Jewish Communists who were manipulating everything from Hollywood to race-relations in a plot to bring down White Christian civilization.

Swift founded his own branch of the Ku Klux Klan, as well as a paramilitary underground.

Now a rising star of the postwar American far-Right, Wesley Swift was making waves across California's political and spiritual landscapes. In 1946 he organized his own Ku Klux Klan faction, the Christian Knights of the Invisible Empire, and staged cross-burnings and paramilitary training in the Antelope Valley desert. More importantly, Swift also founded his own religious denomination, The Church of Jesus Christ—Christian, to disseminate his version of British Israelism, and to be the spiritual arm of his racist, anti-Semitic, and anti-Communist crusade.

The denomination grew steadily throughout California in the 1950s, planting branches in San Francisco, Oakland, Lancaster, Riverside, Hollywood, and San Diego. There was also a Church center in Florida under the Rev. Oren Potito, Swift's East Coast coordinator and an organizer for the National States' Rights Party—a Neo-Nazi/Klan fusionist group whose leaders would later serve time for bombing Black churches and Jewish temples. Swift's own lieutenant and co-preacher, the Rev. Charles "Connie" Lynch, also served as the NSRP's California leader, as well as a "traveling parson" at Klan rallies across the South.

"God Was Calling for Segregation"

Swift's most important associate in California, however, was William Potter Gale. A retired Army Lieutenant Colonel who had organized Filipino guerrillas during World War II, Gale lent a distinctly paramilitary tone to Swift's operations, helping the preacher form the Christian Defense League as an umbrella group for various far-Right religious and political organizations. Gale also started the California Rangers, a secretive guerrilla corps that acted as the Church and League's armed militant wing.

As the Civil Rights movement gained steam, and the Fifties became the Sixties, the rhetoric of Swift, his associates, and his followers, got louder and more strident. Using British-Israelite exegesis, Swift insisted in the booklet *The Mystery of Iniquity* that God had created the races as not only separate but unequal:

> *And God spoke out then, against these Hivites that came out of the Hittites. He spoke out against the Amorites, the Canaanites. He spoke out against the Perizzites,*

the Jebusites. And he told His people not to mix with them, not to have covenants with them, not to intermarry with them, for they would teach His people to serve other gods. They would have no spiritual capacity, and the spirit of God would not cohabit in any of their mixed-blood offspring. Such offspring, He said, would be totally unable to understand the truths of God. So God was calling for segregation!

Jews fared no better in Swift's doctrines. The preacher was quoted as saying "All Jews must be destroyed," and in a 1962 sermon, he stated "the days are going to come when there's not going to be any of them (the JEWS) in the United States either, because the Bible says so in the book of Zechariah .... The destroyers of America (the JEWS) are going to discover that it's not the best place to remain inside of these United States, as America wakes up." Colonel Gale seconded his spiritual leader, ranting, "You got your nigger Jews, you got your Asiatic Jews and you got your white Jews. They're all Jews, and they're all the offspring of the Devil."

"All Jews must be destroyed… (the Jews) are going to discover that it's not the best place to remain inside of these United States, as America wakes up."

Gale, who preached Swift's teachings at his own Ministry of Christ Church in Glendale, later claimed that he coined a new term to describe this White-supremacist form of British-Israelite Adventism: *Christian Identity*. Like many other heterodox Christian doctrines, Christian Identity maintained that apocalyptic Biblical prophecy was being fulfilled in the modern world, and called on its followers to repent and join its struggle against the principalities and powers of evil. Unlike most Christian millenarianism, however, the Identity creed prophesied that its believers would not be raptured into Heaven in the Last Days, but would fight an all-out war against the Communists, the "mud races," and the Jews to establish the Kingdom on Earth.

The Awful Grace of God

Some of Swift's followers took his battle cry to heart. In August 1963, California Ranger George Joseph King Jr., was busted for attempting to sell a .50 caliber machine gun and a British Sten submachine gun to undercover agents. One year later, agents raided the Cucamonga home of Christian Defense League member William H. Garland, and seized nearly 100 arms, including fully-operational machine guns, 105MM rockets, and bomb-making equipment. And in 1965 another Swift follower, Keith Gilbert, was caught with 1,400 pounds of stolen TNT; when asked what the explosives were for, he replied that he planned to blow up the Hollywood Palladium when Rev. Martin Luther King spoke there.

Swift's followers saw the rise of King and the general Sixties *Zeitgeist* as confirmation that the End Times were nigh. Many held "listening parties" in the American South, where far-Right radicals terrified by the end of legal Black segregation and White supremacy gathered to hear Swift's sermons on cassette tapes, and plotted counter-revolution against what they saw as a Godless Communist takeover of the country.

In the book *The Awful Grace of God: Religious Terrorism, White Supremacy, and the Unsolved Murder of Martin Luther King, Jr.*, authors Stuart Wexler and Larry Hancock

Dick DeMarsico

Swift's followers may have planned King's assassination.

> *"[W]hen Dr. Swift spoke, he spoke in Technicolor. The words came out and you could just see in living color what he was talking about. You could—he was a master orator...."*

maintained that Swift's taped sermons brought together an underground Klan/NSRP terror network dedicated to killing the civil-rights leader. This network, they said, had provided James Earl Ray, who would later be convicted of King's assassination, with financial incentive to commit the murder, as well as cover within its ranks. To the authors, Swift was the brains behind—if not an active co-conspirator in—one of the greatest crimes in American history.

Yet back in Lancaster, Swift's physical ministry was fading rapidly. Although the preacher could still fill meeting halls, he wasn't able to hold onto a solid cadre of Californian followers, and his churches across the state folded. Then Gerald L.K. Smith dissociated himself from Swift's organization, and migrated to Eureka Springs, Arkansas, where he built a "religious theme park" that featured a 67 foot-tall statue of Jesus.

Further troubles came when Swift quarreled with William Potter Gale about the Christian Defense League's role in their operations. The Colonel-cum-Reverend split with the Lancaster preacher shortly thereafter, claiming years later that the "pig" Swift had defrauded some of his most loyal followers in an investment deal. Gale continued to preach Christian Identity doctrines at his own Ministry of Christ church, now relocated to a ranch near Mariposa, California.

Aryan Nations

Before his departure, Gale introduced Swift to a middle-aged, Los Angeles-based aerospace engineer who would later make the Church of Jesus Christ—Christian, under an appended name, synonymous with American White-racist crime and terrorism.

The engineer was Richard Girnt Butler, a former member of William Dudley Pelley's Fascist Silver Legion. Later, he joined the California Rangers, and it was Colonel Gale who told Butler that the Lancaster preacher had the goods on who and what was really behind the Reds and their assorted ill-doings.

As Butler recalled years later: "I finally agreed to go [to Swift's church] one time. And I must say, when Dr. Swift spoke, he spoke in Technicolor. The words came out and you could just see in living color what he was talking about. You could—he was a master orator, just a master orator." Independently wealthy from patents and other sources, Butler moved to Palmdale, just south of Swift's ranch in Lancaster, and soon became a force in the now-dwindling California ranks of the Church.

Although he still regularly preached sermons and distributed tapes, by the end of the Sixties Wesley Swift was seriously ill from diabetes, untreated because he distrusted the "Jewish" medical system. When he finally sought American help at a Tijuana clinic, he expired of a heart attack in their waiting

Aryan Nations follower Robert Mathews led The Order: a neo-Nazi terror gang that staged robberies and murders in the Northwest

room on October 8, 1970, aged 57 years. Swift's wife Olive Lorraine continued to distribute his books and tapes until her own death in 2005.

Butler took over as the heir apparent to not only the Church of Jesus Christ—Christian, but also to the multinational network of White racists and radical-Right militants to whom Swift ministered. With Los Angeles rapidly becoming a multiracial and politically liberal city, Butler abandoned Southern California, and moved his family and the Church to a 20-acre ranch near Hayden Lake, Idaho in April 1974.

In Idaho, Butler renamed Swift's organization the Church of Jesus Christ Christian—Aryan Nations, although it would become best known as simply "Aryan Nations." He surrounded himself with paramilitary guards clad in Stormtrooper-style uniforms, who maintained order at Butler's Church services, as well as at the "Aryan Nations World Congresses": annual rallies on the property that attracted hundreds of neo-Nazis, Klansmen, and ultra-Right radicals from across the Western world. At the Congresses, attendees swapped Nazi salutes, burned crosses, and listened to sermons by Butler, whose rhetoric was becoming even more militant than his mentor's in the post-Sixties, racially-integrated America he inhabited and feared.

The Silent Brotherhood

Although Butler was careful to never openly advocate violence, some of his followers formed gangs, and terrorized Jews, people of color, government officials, and other Identity enemies throughout the region. The most notorious of these was "The Silent Brotherhood," or simply, "The Order": an underground neo-Nazi terror gang led by Hayden Lake regular Robert Mathews that staged armed robberies and murders throughout the Northwest until Mathews was cornered and gunned down by police at Whidbey Island, Washington on December 8, 1984.

After the Whidbey Island siege, Federal, state and local law enforcement started a campaign of surveillance and infiltration of the Hayden Lake compound. And when Aryan Nations security guards assaulted a woman and her son in 1998, the Southern Poverty Law Center, a nonprofit organization that monitors American "hate groups", took the Church to court on her behalf, and won a $6.3 million judgment against them in 2001. Bankrupted, the Church surrendered its Hayden Lake center and other assets.

Back in California, former Wesley Swift associate William Potter Gale's Christian-Identity ministry also collapsed under government pressure. In 1986, Federal officials, who had linked Gale's paramilitary "Committee of the States" to illegal doings, raided his 100-acre Manasseh Ranch, arrested the frail 70 year-old Colonel, and charged him and several associates with conspiracy to overthrow the government and murder its employees. Although convicted, the ailing Gale avoided Federal imprisonment, and died on April 28, 1988. With his passing, his ministry faded into history.

Although Richard Butler himself was eventually deposed from Aryan Nations leadership in a political struggle, he remained the spiritual head of the Christian Identity movement—a celebrity in the White-racist subculture who stayed active until his death at 86 in 2004.

Today at least three separate factions, based in Louisiana, New York State, and South Carolina, claim leadership of the Aryan Nations remnant. Judging by their Web sites and news reports, most are composed of hard-bitten ex-cons, outlaw bikers, racist skinheads, and others from the criminal fringes of American society—a far cry from the lower-middle-class White-Californian squares Swift harangued in Christian Identity's early years.

Still, whether its tenets are shouted on the cell block, preached in country churches, or downloaded from the Internet, the Lancaster pastor's doctrines will no doubt continue to speak to alienated and angry White Americans ready to see in themselves, as Swift did, a Chosen People being chastised by their Lord for their impiety and sinfulness. Whether one sees in Christian Identity a clarion-call to a people dispossessed of a distinct spiritual and cultural identity, or a demented and dangerous warrant for terror in God's name, one must acknowledge how well Swift and his followers re-invented the Old Testament mythos of the oppressed-yet-superior *Holy Tribe* for consumption in a racially-divided modern nation.

10
Jack T. Chick
& His Comic-Book Ministry

Rancho Cucamonga's Jack T. Chick may be the most influential Christian evangelist of the modern world. Yet his ministry is contained in no church building, carried on no airwaves, and isn't even incorporated as a religious organization.

JimmyAkin.com

JIMMY AKIN

Artist's rendition of Jack T. Chick

Rather, Jack Chick is the artist, writer and publisher behind Chick Publications, home of the so-called "Chick comics" or "Chick tracts." These are miniature evangelical comic books that feature both an ultra-Fundamentalist Christian message, and some of the most lurid themes and graphics ever created in the name of Christ.

Since 1962, over 800 million of these little tracts have been produced and distributed. In terms of sheer numbers, Chick is the most widely-read living author on earth, and his tracts' influence in the Christian literary world is second only to the Holy Bible itself.

That influence has made Chick and his works one of the most controversial topics in Christian evangelism. Are the tracts simple and cost-efficient, yet hugely effective ways to bring the Good News to total strangers? Or do they misrepresent the Christian message with scare tactics and outright falsehoods, and ultimately alienate more people from the Gospel than they attract?

This Was Your Life!

Chick is an L.A. native, a World War II veteran, and a technical illustrator who accepted Jesus Christ as his Lord and Savior during a late-1940s broadcast of Charles E. Fuller's *Old Fashioned Revival Hour* radio program. Although he wanted to be a missionary, his wife dissuaded him from field work, and he saw himself as too shy to be a proper witness for the Gospel. How, he wondered, could he win souls for Christ?

The answer came in the 1950s, when he heard a radio missionary discussing Chinese communist propaganda. According to the missionary, the Red Chinese noted how popular comic books were in the United States, so they created their own versions: mass-produced and —distributed illustrated tracts that simply and forcefully taught Maoist doctrine to children and marginally-literate peasants.

Chick, who had drawn cartoons since childhood, wondered if this tactic could be applied to Christian evangelism. So he borrowed money from his credit union, and got to work creating and self-publishing small comic-booklets with Evangelical/Fundamentalist themes, designed to be printed and distributed *en masse*—anonymously, if need be.

Chick's first tract appeared in 1960. Four years later, he produced his most popular title, *This Was Your Life!*—the story of a high-living swinger who's felled by a heart attack, and carried by an angel to the Great White Throne. There a faceless God confronts him, berates him for his sin-drenched life, and tosses him into the Lake of Fire. A second story follows, showing how the man might have lived had he dedicated himself to Christ, and concludes with his ascent to Heaven. Reportedly 65 million copies of the tract have been printed over the last 50 years.

Since 1962, over 800 million "Chick Comics" have been produced and distributed.

Over 65 million copies of this Chick tract in print.

Chick's artistic and literary styles have remained unchanged since the early 1960s. His drawings ape the pop-eyed, sweaty-browed, wildly-gesticulating characters of classic Sunday-funnies, and his conniving demons and villains inevitably rub their hands together and cackle "Haw! Haw!" in Saturday-matinee bad-guy style. Speech-bubbles and thought-balloons narrate the action, and obscenities are blipped out with jumbles of punctuation marks.

Although Chick has never acknowledged it, his tracts bear a striking resemblance to "Tijuana Bibles." These were small comic books, popular from the 1920s to the 1960s, that featured cartoon characters or movie stars in explicitly pornographic stories. The "Bibles" were palm-sized, crudely-drawn, reveled in stereotypes and caricatures, and were distributed largely to children, adolescents, and the unlettered—all characteristics that Chick's tracts share.

And like the pornographic comic-books, there's little thematic variation in Chick's tracts. Most of them present stories about protagonists who either accept Jesus as Lord and Savior and find peace and heavenly immortality, or reject Him, and get tossed into a dime-store-Dante Hell of flame-belching caverns and leering demons. Some set up confrontations between bearers of False Doctrines and exponents of King-James-Bible-Only Fundamentalist Christianity, with the latter inevitably winning the debates, and sometimes the souls, of their opponents.

The Bull, Bad Bob, and Lisa

Subtlety and nuance are nowhere to be found in the twenty-odd-page mini-comics. The Bad Guys, be they liberals, evolutionists, or unrepentant sinners, are always depicted as ugly brutes, angry fanatics, or clueless stooges, and are inevitably motivated by greed, stupidity, perversity, sheer evil, or some combination thereof. The Good Guys are, without exception, clear-featured and calm Every(wo)men who want only to save souls from the eternal torment guaranteed to any human not personally accepting Jesus as their savior. And there are always cartoon demons lurking around the action, whispering temptations into the ears of innocent dupes, and sometimes even wholly possessing the bodies of Freemasons, Mormons, drug addicts, or other unsavory characters.

Chick's tracts bear a striking resemblance to the pornographic "Tijuana Bibles" of yesteryear.

Like the God he serves, Jack T. Chick is no respecter of persons. In his comic yarns, often the most depraved, degenerate characters end up redeemed, while the most seemingly righteous ones are condemned. In the prison setting of *The Bull*, a behemoth, murderous psychopath finds a Chick tract in the solitary hole, repents of his sins, and then strong-arms both fellow prisoners and guards into fellowship with Christ. In *Bad Bob*, a brutal, drug-dealing outlaw-biker violently rejects an evangelist, only to later beg his spiritual help when a jail fire nearly kills him. And in the withdrawn comic *Lisa*, a dad molests his preteen daughter and infects her with an STD, but is brought to Christ by her examining doctor.

On the other hand, the elderly missionary couple who perish on *Flight 144* are thrown into the Lake of Fire despite their fifty years' of building schools and hospitals, and serving the Third World poor. In Chick's world, selfless altruism and good works count for nothing, if one hasn't turned oneself over to the Lord using his formulaic prayer, conveniently printed on the back page of all the tracts:

1. *Admit you are a sinner. See Romans 3:10*
2. *Be willing to turn from sin (repent). See Acts 17:30*
3. *Believe that Jesus Christ died for you, was buried and rose from the dead. See Rom. 10:9-10*
4. *Through prayer, invite Jesus into your life to become your personal Saviour. See Rom. 10:13*

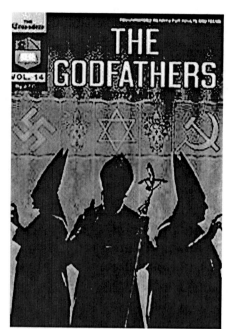

Chick's Alberto series claimed the Catholic Church was behind Communism, Nazism, and other evils

The Death Cookie

Among all the various bogeymen that appear in Chick's tracts, one entity not only dominates and controls all the others, but is the very Antichrist that will bring about the Apocalypse through its depredations. In Jack T. Chick's universe, The Roman Catholic Church is Spiritual Enemy #1 to true Bible-believing Christians, and the comic-books bash the Papacy and its works with a righteous, relentless fury.

In the tract *The Death Cookie*, Chick maintained that the Eucharist was invented by scheming Satanist infiltrators, and depicted tiny demons living in Communion Hosts. In *Is There Another Christ?* he charged that the Pope and the Catholic priesthood are blasphemous usurpers of Jesus Christ's role as Savior. And in *Why is Mary Crying?* he claimed that Marian devotions lead Catholics away from true worship of her Son.

Chick's Catholic-baiting reached a crescendo in his *Alberto* series. These were large-sized, full-color graphic novels that illustrated the life and testimony of Alberto Rivera, a Canary Islands native who claimed to have been a former Jesuit priest tasked to infiltrate and destroy Protestant churches and institutions. Although he was rewarded with a Bishopric for his efforts, Rivera saw the error of his ways in the mid-1960s, converted to Fundamentalist Christianity, and dedicated himself to exposing Rome's machinations.

Rivera and Chick charged that the Roman Catholic Church created Islam, the Freemasons, the Illuminati, the Mafia, Mormonism, the Jehovah's Witnesses, the Ku Klux Klan, New Age spirituality, Communism, Nazism, and the Christian ecumenical movement, and uses these disparate groups to enforce its edicts and sow discord among true Christians. Most alarmingly, they claimed that the Vatican had inspired the Holocaust, and was planning to exterminate a half-billion Protestants during the End Times.

> *Chick and Rivera claimed the Catholic Church plan to exterminate a half-billion Protestants during the End Times.*

Even by the standards of historical anti-Papist rhetoric, Rivera and Chick's charges were outrageous, self-contradictory, and easily refuted by scholars. But millions of readers believed them, and Evangelical Christian bookstores began to stock the *Alberto* series and other anti-Catholic Chick works. Alarmed, some Christian journalists began to cast critical looks at Rivera and Chick.

Christianity Today's Gary Metz discovered that while working for Tennessee's Church of God of Prophecy, Rivera had swindled a Spanish Evangelical college, and was wanted in Florida and New Jersey for fraud. Rivera had claimed to have been a celibate Jesuit priest during the early 1960s, but records revealed that he'd been a married father of three and an employee of the ultra-Protestant Christian Reformed Church at that time. Metz also found no conclusive evidence that Rivera had ever been a Roman Catholic cleric, much less a "Jesuit bishop," and was refused an interview with the self-described ex-priest.

In response, Chick said that Rivera was the victim of an ongoing smear- and framing-campaign by the Vatican, and stood by the charges made in the *Alberto* series. Rivera ended up pastoring a Hispanic Evangelical church in Oxnard, California until his death in 1997.

Bride of Satan

The success of the *Alberto* titles led Chick into full-length book publishing. In the mid-1980s, Chick produced two books by Rebecca Brown, *He Came to Set the Captives Free,* and *Prepare for War*. A former doctor, Brown told the story of Elaine, a patient of hers who claimed she had not only been initiated into a large, powerful Satanic coven, but had become a "Regional Bride of Satan," and had accompanied the Adversary himself on international missions to sell arms, network with allies like the Pope and the Freemasons, and generally spread discord across the Earth.

Somehow, Elaine ended up at Dr. Brown's hospital, where the physician exorcised her many demons, and ultimately turned her to Christ. Elaine joined the good Doctor in her crusade against Satan's minions, and after a series of violent retaliations from the forces of darkness put them on the run, the two took their story to Jack T. Chick.

He Came To Set The Captives Free

By Rebecca Brown, MD

Rebecca Brown's Satan-fighting books were bestsellers.

Again, skeptical journalists investigated the stories. One report revealed that Dr. Brown was the former Ruth Irene Bailey, an Indiana physician who'd been ejected from a hospital residency for denouncing her fellow M.D.s as "demons, devils and other evil spirits," and who'd lost her medical license for narcotics addiction. "Elaine" had been Edna Elaine Moses, a nurse with a long history of mental illness and drug addiction, with whom the physician had shared a home and bed.

Eventually Dr. Bailey and Ms. Moses surfaced in Apple Valley, California, where they reinvented themselves as "Rebecca Brown" and "Elaine," and told their stories to Jack T. Chick. Unaware of their backgrounds, and untroubled by the absence of solid evidence they gave to back up their wild assertions, Chick published their testimonies first as cassette tapes, then as full-length books.

It was a profitable move. America was at the height of the 1980s' "Satanic Ritual Abuse" scare, and Brown's books found a ready audience among Americans willing to believe that devil-worship was widespread, well-organized, and sacrificing innocent people by the truckload. The two women even appeared on Geraldo Rivera's sensationalist talk-show in 1987—a publicity coup for Chick Publications that put Brown's works on evangelical-Christian bestseller lists.

Chick author John Todd claimed that he'd been in the Illuminati with Billy Graham and Jerry Falwell.

Soon, however, Chick's promoters of the "Satanic Ritual Abuse" legend began to strain credulity past the breaking point. When Chick author John Todd claimed that he'd formerly been a leader of the Satanic "Illuminati," and named Billy Graham, Jerry Falwell, and other well-known Evangelical figures as members, Christian investigative-journalists revealed that Todd was an inveterate liar, criminal, and drug-addict with documented mental illnesses. The alleged ex-Illuminist lost most of his audience, and he eventually died while on parole for a rape conviction.

As the Satanic-panic waned, Chick quietly distanced himself from the Munchausenesque fabulists in his stable. He let Rebecca Brown's books go out of print, and expunged some of the more outlandish claims from his comics, such as John Todd's assertion that 40,000 Americans are murdered every year in Witchcraft rites. He also updated other tracts to deal with new evils ranging from AIDS to the *Family Guy* TV show, and produced "Black" and "Asian" versions of *This Was Your Life!* and other popular tracts to appeal to an increasingly multiracial audience.

The Light of the World

By the 21st century, Chick's readership, and the business that catered to it, had expanded to considerable proportions. His Rancho Cucamonga-based Chick Publications employed over 35 people, and took in over $3 million a year, mostly from sales to churches, youth groups and individuals. The tracts and comic books have been translated into over 100 languages, and are endlessly distributed, discussed, analyzed, praised, criticized, and parodied by a vast religious and secular audience.

In recent years, Chick's audience has included a fair number of people who ignore or reject his evangelical message, but are fascinated by his comics' primitive style and crude propagandistic power. To them, the Chick tracts are a peek into the mind of Evangelical Christianity at its most dumbed-down, paranoid, and intolerant, and carry the frisson of the forbidden formerly associated with pornography. A creative few have produced clever parodies of the tracts, using the mini-comic format and simple cartoon-styles to promote such manifestly un-Chickian ideologies as Evolutionism, Neo-Paganism, and psychedelics-based spirituality.

For all his combined fame and notoriety, Chick himself has remained something of an enigma. True to his retiring character, he's given only one formal interview since 1975, and avoids cameras. His reclusive nature has just added to the mystique of Chick Publications, leading some to speculate that "Jack T. Chick" was a pseudonym for a collective of Evangelical cartoonists.

One journalist who did manage to locate and speak with the elusive Chick was Catholic writer Jimmy Akin. When *The Light of the World*, a Chick-produced motion picture, premiered at an Ontario, California theatre in 2004, Akin dropped by, and noticed a paunchy, bespectacled, white-haired man in the audience greeting well-wishers. Sure enough, it was the one and only Jack T. Chick.

Chick chortled with laughter when Akin introduced himself as an employee of Catholic Answers, an apologist organization that's tirelessly critiqued Chick's Vatican-bashing tracts. The two chatted amiably and parted cordially, although Chick added ominously, "We're in the war. I'm sure we'll be hearing from you in the future."

"We're in the war. I'm sure we'll be hearing from you in the future."

And no doubt, the world at large will be hearing from Jack T. Chick as long as his earthly mission endures. Now in his nineties, Chick continues to steward his small but hugely influential publishing empire, which now sports a sophisticated Web site that offers previews and online-embedding of his tracts, extensive FAQ pages that explain his teachings and opinions, and DVDs and e-Books alongside the hardcopy tracts and tomes.

Perhaps the most revealing page on the site is Chick's "Special Message," where he recounts how his friends never witnessed to him in high school, because they felt he could

A collector's guide to Chick Tracts.

never receive Christ's thruth. When he considered that he might have been killed in World War II and sent straight to Hell, Chick related:

> *...I was speechless. I felt betrayed. If I had died, my blood would have been on their hands.*
>
> *I wonder how many souls I've overlooked and neglected: neighbors, friends, etc. It's an awesome thought. Ezekiel 3:18 says, "When I say unto the wicked, Thou shalt surely die; and thou givest him not warning, nor speakest to warn the wicked from his wicked way, to save his life; the same wicked man shall die in his iniquity; but his blood will I require at thine hand." That is an awesome verse.*
>
> *May God give us a greater burden to reach the dying world, and to remember we will give an account at the Judgment Seat of Christ for what we did down here.*

At that heavenly Judgment Seat, will God praise Chick for his tireless, global-scale evangelism? Will He damn him for his unapologetic promotion of false witnesses and questionable doctrines? Or will He view him and his works as so many mortals do—with a mixture of fascination, repulsion and amusement—and in His infinite wisdom consign the cartoonist to some unimaginable fate, suitable solely for the man whose 50-year career made Rancho Cucamonga a world center for comic-book Christian evangelism?

Only Heaven knows.

11

R.L. Hymers & the Fundamentalist Army

On July 16, 1988, the high tide of American Fundamentalist Christianity crashed onto the shores of Tinseltown. That day, Dr. Robert Leslie Hymers Jr., the 47 year-old, ultra-conservative Baptist pastor and founder of the Fundamentalist Army and various other ministries, took 200 of his followers to North Hollywood, where they formed a picket line in front of the MCA/Universal studio lot entrance.

Incensed by the studio's upcoming release of *The Last Temptation of Christ*—a film whose allegedly blasphemous contents had already ignited a firestorm of controversy across the Christian world—the protestors unfurled a huge banner that read, "[MCA Chairman Lew] Wasserman Fans Hatred toward the Jews with 'Temptation' Movie." Others held up placards with caricatures of Wasserman and Stars of David, bearing slogans like "Wasserman Endangers Israel." In the sky overhead, a small plane trailed a banner that blamed the MCA chief for inciting anti-Jewish hatred.

The Rev. Dr. R.L. Hymers

The international media, which had covered the controversy over the film, was stunned by the demonstration. By calling attention to the studio head's Jewishness, the protestors seemed to be fanning the flames of the anti-Semitism they claimed to oppose. And many Jews in the film industry were alarmed at what looked like an eruption of anti-Semitic agitation in their own backyard.

Soon, reporters got busy investigating the background of Hymers and his ominously-named "Fundamentalist Army" ministry. What they found was a story of a highly-educated pastor with an eclectic theology, hundreds of "house church"-based followers throughout Southern California, a knack for generating publicity and controversy, and a community of critics who maintained he ran an abusive and hateful cult.

Bickering, Drinking, Swearing

Hymers was a California native, born in Glendale on April 12, 1941, and raised in a family filled with "bickering, drinking, swearing—just a home life that no child should be subjected to," according to a neighbor who took the troubled youth under his wing, and brought him to church. At 13, Hymers embraced Christ; four years later he heard the call to preach the Gospel.

Although he was originally licensed to preach by Huntington Beach's First Southern Baptist Church, the teenaged evangelist got his real training under Dr. Timothy Lin—a hard-shell Biblical-inerrancy advocate who schooled the young minister in orthodox Baptist theology and homiletics. Eventually Hymers graduated from California State University, and went on to earn Doctorates of Religion, Ministry, Theology, and Literature from four other institutions.

Ordained by Dr. Lin in July 1972, Hymers founded Mill Valley's Church of the Open Door, a nondenominational group that eventually became a Southern Baptist church. In 1975 he planted a second church in Los Angeles: Westwood's Maranatha Chapel, later to be known as The Open Door Community Churches of Los Angeles.

"Drink Like Melchisidech and Jesus."

Hymers felt that Western Christianity had become institutionalized and stagnant, and needed to return to its First-Century roots as a semi-underground movement where members hosted congregations in their own homes. These houses would be communal-living situations where Christians could live cheaply, support each other's spiritual growth, and collectively raise children in the faith.

During the 1970s his Los Angeles ministry established a network of these house-churches throughout the region.

Hymers "dropped and barred" followers who displeased him, publicly reading them out of the movement at Sunday services.

Hymers also added distinctly non-Baptist practices to his early ministry. One was "deliverance ministry" of new converts—the casting out demons and unclean spirits that had occupied their bodies. Another was "singing in the Spirit"—a stream-of-consciousness group chant, often accompanied by Pentecostal-style speaking in tongues. During this era, he even approved of moderate drinking for stressed-out faithful, and once preached a sermon on the subject titled, "Drink Like Melchisidech and Jesus—Not Like Erring Noah."

Hymers' house-churches were supervised by "house preachers." These were subordinate pastors who oversaw house activities, held daily prayer meetings and Sunday-morning services, and organized "Gideon's Army"—a door-to-door evangelical campaign that brought converts into the Church's orbit. House preachers also kept track of turnout and participation at all house meetings and activities, and reported absentees and slackers to Hymers, who forcefully rebuked them either in person, or from the pulpit at the Church's Sunday services. The public-shaming kept doubters and dissenters in line, and guaranteed near-perfect attendance at most Church functions.

The Big Push

Obsessed with numerical growth, Hymers planned to double his following in size annually. In his plan, each house-church preacher would grow his or her community to at least 60 members, and train at least one other member in pastoral duties. When this goal was reached, the community would split, cell-like, into two house-churches under separate pastors, each of whom would be responsible for repeating the process.

"Pray for Death: Baby-Killer Brennan."

Hymers' house-preachers were hard-pressed to keep up with the exponential-growth model. Undaunted, in late 1980 Hymers announced the "Big Push"—an all-out, ten-week campaign to meet the 100%-annual growth goal. Although the campaign worked, and the Church boasted 1,200 members by the end of the year, it strained the house-preachers' evangelical abilities to their limits, and brought in hundreds of casual converts not fully committed to the house-church lifestyle.

By this point, the Church had taken on a distinctly ecumenical tone. Christians from all denominational backgrounds were welcome in the Open Door Community so long as they attended the house functions and the Sunday rallies. This approach vastly increased his potential pool of recruits, and made the Church's annual-doubling goal viable, at least on paper.

But all was not well in Hymers' modest ecclesiastical empire. The "Big Push" campaign had burned out his already-overworked house-preachers, many of whom defected. Their posts were taken by in-house-trained leaders who loyally carried out Hymers' orders, strengthening the Church's chain of command.

Hymers also regularly "dropped and barred" followers who displeased him, publicly reading them out of the movement at Sunday services, and forbidding any contact between them and the faithful. By the mid-1980s, his flock dwindled to 300-400 hardcore followers.

The Fundamentalist Army

Around this time, Hymers also changed his church's name and theology. His ministry was no longer called The Open Door Community Church, and the ecumenical approach of earlier years was abandoned. Now the group would be known as The Fundamentalist Army, and Hymers began to preach hell-and-damnation sermons that condemned the world outside his sect as irreparably sinful. He also ordered his followers to shun not only ex-Church members, but any friends or family members not wholly sympathetic to the ministry.

Hymers also reorganized his sect. He eliminated the house-preacher office in favor of lay stewards who ran the house-churches, and dutifully played tapes of their leader's sermons at group meetings. This effectively centralized all power under Hymers—a move that alarmed ex-Hymerites, who had by now organized an informal support group where they debriefed defectors and compared notes.

By the mid-1980s, Hymers had become L.A.'s most visible Fundamentalist Christian leader. He often publicized his sermons with lurid posters and flyers, such as one that sported a photo of Marilyn Monroe with the headline, "SEX AFTER DEATH?" and another with John Lennon that read, "DEAD BEATLE SPEAKS! SEX AND DRUGS! DON'T MISS HIS MES-SAGE!" A former journalism student, Hymers knew that nothing worked like star-power, scandal, and sensation to snag the masses' increasingly-distracted attentions.

Hymers on John Lennon, sex, and drugs

L.A.'s Fundamentalist Army made national headlines in June 1986, when U.S. Supreme Court Justice William J. Brennan spoke at Loyola Marymount University's commencement ceremony. During the speech, a Hymers-hired airplane buzzed overhead towing a banner that read: "Pray for Death: Baby-Killer Brennan"—a reference to the Justice's ruling on 1973's Roe v. Wade case, which effectively legalized abortion throughout the USA. Days later, Hymers held a special Sunday meeting of the faithful to petition the Lord for Brennan's demise, and led a noisy "Pray for the Death of Pro-Death Court" rally in front of Los Angeles' U.S. District Court building. Although local pro-life leaders admired Hymers' fervor, they distanced themselves from his rhetoric and tactics, and said that praying for the death of individuals was decidedly rash, if not un-Christian.

Hymers made the news again in April 1988, when La Mirada's evangelical-Christian Biola University announced it that its students could now drink, smoke, gamble, and—worst of all—dance to rock music when off-campus. A onetime Biola student, Hymers told the *Los Angeles Times* that the university's policy "is part of a moral slide that marks both the decline of our civilization and the end of this age," and attacked school officials and defended his Puritanical views on local news broadcasts.

"A Bad Movie about Jesus"

A few weeks later, Hymers jumped into the center of a controversy that drew battle lines between cultural "conservatives" and "liberals" across the globe.

Months before the August 1988 release of the film *The Last Temptation of Christ,* pirated versions of the screenplay found their way to various Christian leaders, who were troubled by its portrayal of a Jesus beset by self-doubt, confusion, and temptation. Especially disturbing to orthodox believers was a sequence where, during His time on the Cross, Satan transports Jesus to an alternate reality where He consummates a marriage to Mary Magdalene—the crowning blasphemy in what many Christians felt was a deadly cinematic insult to their faith. With the film still weeks away from release, Evangelical Christian and Roman Catholic leaders organized letter-writing campaigns and boycotts against Universal Studios/MCA, and other firms and individuals connected with the film.

"These Jewish people bankroll a film that makes Jesus look insane."

But it was the pugnacious, publicity-hungry Reverend Hymers who took Christian opprobrium to the next level. On July 18th he staged the rally in front of Universal Studios that put him in news reports around the world, and injected what many felt was an anti-Semitic tone into the controversy.

When reporters asked Hymers why he thought Wasserman endangered Jews, he replied, "These Jewish producers with a lot of money are taking a swipe at our religion. Of course, it's going to cause a backlash." Hymers, who maintained that Wasserman was alienating the Christian community from Jews and Israel, also forbid journalists from interviewing any members of his picketing flock, saying that although "they know there's a bad movie about Jesus" afoot, some of them might not be able to tell why or even who they were protesting.

Two days later, Hymers upped the ante, holding a demonstration not fifty yards from Wasserman's home in Beverly Hills. As his supporters held signs claiming that *Temptation* was "Paid with Jewish Money!" Hymers told the assembled media: "There should be an outcry from the Christian community when these Jewish people bank-roll a film that makes Jesus look insane...It's dangerous for the Jewish people to have this film put out." Hymers drove home his point with a bit of street theater: one of his followers, costumed as Jesus Christ and spattered with fake blood, lugged an eight-foot wooden cross down the tree-lined street, only to be kicked to the ground by a suit-clad, bloody-handed actor who represented Wasserman.

The protests provoked outrage on both sides of the controversy. Jewish organizations ranging from the B'nai B'rith to the Jewish Defense League pillo-ried Hymers and his church, saying that his rhetoric was encouraging the very anti-Semitism he claimed to oppose. Undaunted, Hymers led yet more protests against the film at Los Angeles' Wilshire Boulevard Temple and Jewish Community Center, as well as follow-up pickets at Wasserman's home.

The pastor rode his newfound national notori-ety to an appearance on CNN's *Crossfire* program, where he debated liberal Baptist Reverend Robert Thompson about the film. Hymers promised anoth-er reporter that a release of the film would start a "war," but the best he could muster when *Temptation*

Movie poster: The Last Temptation of Christ

finally hit the screen was another rally outside the Universal lot, where he and his followers staged a crucifixion of Wasserman in effigy.

The demonstrations attracted little new blood into the Fundamentalist Army, and virtually no sympathy from the media. Instead, they alienated friends and allies, many of whom saw Hymers' rhetoric and tactics as tasteless, if not blatantly anti-Semitic. Local Jewish, Catholic, and Protestant leaders alike condemned the Fundamentalist leader, and questioned his seeming obsession with the studio head's Jewishness. Confronted with their reactions, Hymers backed off, said he "didn't want anything to do with anti-Semitism," and apologized if anyone interpreted his words or actions as hateful.

A Church on the Fringe

But some behind-the-scenes accounts seemed to confirm Hymers' alleged anti-Semitism, as well as his rumored mistreatment of followers. *The Los Angeles Times* ran a series of articles about the pastor where ex-Church members claimed he called his Jewish converts "kikes" on a regular basis, and beat and psychologically abused his followers. Local news-station KCOP broadcast a three-part expose on Hymers that featured interviews with former faithful, who maintained that the pastor tried to control every aspect of his followers' lives, and publically humiliated them for seemingly minor transgressions. Hymers himself vociferously denied the charges, pointing to his many devoted followers and dismissing the stories of abuse.

But Hymers found it harder to ignore a report about his church by Ronald Enroth, a prominent Evangelical author and sociologist who specialized in the study of marginal Christian sects. In an *Eternity* magazine article called "Churches on the Fringe," Enroth maintained that Hymers' movement was one of several cult-like, authoritarian Christian groups that had emerged in modern America, and corroborated many of the accounts of abuse. Eventually, Enroth compiled his findings about the Fundamentalist Army and other sects into a full-

> *"I made a terrible mistake. What I did was wrong and I apologize for it."*

length book, *Churches That Abuse*, which became a classic study of Christian-sectarian extremism.

Faced with widespread criticism, and saddled with a Church that wasn't exactly setting Los Angeles aflame spiritually, Hymers reorganized and renamed his ministry once more. Abandoning the house-churches, he purchased a building at 1329 South Hope Street in downtown Los Angeles, and dubbed it the Fundamentalist Baptist Temple—the centralized, non-residential heart of Hymers' sect.

In the post-*Temptation* era, Hymers also worked to mend relations with the Jewish community. In a 1992 interview with the *Jerusalem Post,* the pastor recalled his anti-Wasserman demonstrations and admitted "I made a terrible mistake. What I did was wrong and I apologize for it." That year, Hymers joined a group of over 200 Christian clergy who pledged to preach an annual sermon on the evils of anti-Semitism, and in support of Israel and the Jews. The contrite pastor also apologized for the 1988 "death prayer" against Justice Brennan, although he stressed that he still opposed abortion and would work for its abolition.

One of Hymers' more ironically-themed books

During the 1990s Hymers turned his attentions and energies to the printed page. To date he has penned over fifteen books, ranging from works on Christian theology and apologetics, to studies of UFOs and predictions of a second Holocaust.

Breaking a 30-Year Silence

Hymers briefly blipped onto the national scene once more in early 2006, when libertarian writer Joy McCann broke nearly 30 years of silence to recount her experiences of abuse, mind-control, and rape—at the age of 14—in Hymers' flock. When her accounts appeared online, Hymers' son Robert Hymers III not only threatened McCann with legal retribution, but even reported her to the FBI as a potential terrorist.

But the Feds and courts were uninterested and McCann stood her ground. Eventually Hymers III quit his campaign when a grand jury indicted the 27 year-old accountant for grand theft auto, identity theft, and fraud.

Recent observers who've journeyed to the Fundamentalist Baptist Tabernacle say that Hymers' following seems to be leaner than ever. They claim that fewer than 100 people regularly attend Sunday services at the church—a far cry from the thousand-plus audiences Hymers worked during the glory days of the 1980s, when house-churches seemed to be at the cutting-edge of Christian evangelism, and the outspoken pastor was a regular on the Los Angeles airwaves and front pages. Now in his seventies, Hymers nevertheless still pursues his vision of a doctrinally-pure Church, the heir to both a decidedly-mixed personal legacy, and a fiery American spiritual tradition that's established a small but durable beachhead on the streets of Southern California.

> *Ex-Church members claimed Hymers called Jewish converts "kikes," and beat and psychologically abused his followers.*

12

Harold Camping, Family Radio & the End of the World

Since ancient times, prophets have predicted *The End of the World*. The bolder ones have specified exact times and dates when God would wipe the planet clean of *Homo sapiens*, and render all our doings as mere vanities, and dust in the winds of Eternity.

When their chosen Doomsdays have inevitably come and gone without the predicted natural and spiritual upheavals, some especially nervy seers have assured their followers that they miscalculated the date and/or were misinterpreted, and that *Gotterdammerung* is *still* coming—*really soon*.

A few prophets of doom have had the sheer, brazen

Alameda's Prophet of Doom—Harold Camping

cojones to promise their faithful two successive Days of Rapture… and when both have failed to happen, insist that a *third* date would be the absolute, positive, guaranteed time for the Lord to call all His children home.

Possibly the only historical doomsayer to successfully convince sizable flocks that the Second Coming was due on *four* different occasions was Alameda's Harold Camping. And he did it not in the Dark Ages, nor even in one of America's historical, faith-drunk "Great Awakenings," but in the late-20th and 21st Centuries, whilst seated squarely in one of the world's prime centers of cultural sophistication and religious skepticism—the San Francisco Bay Area.

Adam When?

Born in 1921, Camping was a UC Berkeley graduate, a father of seven, and a popular Bible teacher at Alameda's First Christian Reformed Church. An engineer by trade, Camping helped found Alameda-based Family Radio, one of America's first exclusively-Christian broadcast networks, in 1958.

By 1961, Camping had inserted himself into Family Radio's programming. Every weekend, he hosted a call-in show called "Open Forum," where he used his Bible-study knowledge and skill to instruct listeners in the intricacies of Scripture. Camping interpreted Biblical passages and answered callers' questions with the skill and aplomb of a master, effortlessly cross-referencing the King James Version's chapters and verses.

Camping calculated that God had created the Universe in 11,013 B.C.

Camping spent the Sixties running a construction firm by day, hosting "Open Forum" on weekends, studying the Bible relentlessly and working out a complex interpretation of its chronology. In 1970, the Christian American Scientific Association's *Journal* published his paper, "The Biblical Calendar of History," where Camping revealed that he'd finally solved the mysteries of the *Genesis* timeline that had perplexed and frustrated Scriptural scholars for centuries.

In the controversial paper, Camping maintained that Bishop Ussher's famous literalist Bible chronology, which dated the Creation to 4004 B.C. and the Flood to 2349 B.C., "agree[s] neither with the Biblical nor the secular evidence," and was based on a misunderstanding of Scriptural terminology. He instead calculated that the Creation happened in 11,013 B.C., and the Flood in 4990 B.C.—considerably farther back than Ussher or his successors had thought, but still a far cry from mainstream scienctific and theological estimates. Camping elaborated on his findings in a self-published 1974 book titled *Adam When?* but it attracted little notice in Christian circles.

The First Day of Reckoning

By the 1980s, Camping had sold his construction business, and joined Family Radio as President and General Manager. His preaching had taken a distinctly apocalyptic tone; heavily influenced by Evangelical author Edgar

Dozens of Camping's followers gathered in Alameda, waiting for the Rapture and Apocalypse.

Whisenant's books, which asserted that various code words and numerical formulas in Scripture revealed that the end of the world was nigh, Camping maintained that the Apocalypse was due in a few short years, and that the faithful would soon be lifted up to Heaven in an ascension very much like Jesus Christ's after the Resurrection.

His preaching alarmed the elders at Alameda Christian Reformed Church, who asked Camping not to teach any more Bible classes. Incensed, Camping walked out of the congregation, followed by over 100 faithful who preferred his newfound doomsday-doctrines to the Church's historical teachings. The new group met weekly at Alameda's Veterans Memorial Building, where they dedicated themselves to unraveling the mysteries of Holy Writ under Camping's leadership.

Finally, on September 10, 1992, Camping announced on "Open Forum" that after a lifetime of Bible study, he had figured out the exact timeline for Judgment Day. He told his listeners that the "Tribulation" had begun in 1988, but that rather than being a time of God's wrath and torment, it was instead one where true Christians would be abandoned by their false-Gospel preaching churches. As for the Rapture, it would start on Septem-

ber 6, 1994, and culminate nine
to eleven days later, after which
would come Judgment Day, the
End of Times, and the return of
Christ to Earth.

To explain his prediction,
Camping self-published his own
dense book of Biblical-numero-
logical scholarship, *1994?* In it,
Camping maintained that the use
of numbers in Scripture reflected
the symmetrical perfection of
God's creation, and when interpreted properly, revealed His
plans and dates for the End Times.
Although Camping carefully quoted *Matthew 24:36,* saying that "no
man knows the day nor the hour"
of the Second Coming, he felt sure
he'd come within a fortnight of the
exact Day of Reckoning.

*Albrecht Dürer's fif-
teenth-century vision of
the Christian Apocalypse.*

Promoted heavily on Family Radio and in Christian bookstores, *1994?* brought over $1 million in sales revenue to the radio network, which was expanding rapidly, adding new stations and reaching an international audience via satellite. The mainstream secular media took notice as well; no less a figure than Larry King quizzed Camping on his CNN television show about Biblical numerology, and his near-absolute certainty that 9/6/1994 was Doomsday.

On the morning of September 6th, dozens of Camping's followers gathered at the Alameda Veteran's Memorial Building, anxiously awaiting their rapture from a doomed planet. Many brought their children, dressed in their Sunday best. Some Campingites even held open Bibles in their laps, the Holy Scripture facing upwards to their anticipated place of delivery.

But the day came and passed like any other.

The Great Tribulation

Confronted about the failed prediction, Camping replied that he'd mistakenly used the Roman calendar to calculate the date of Apocalypse. Using the Biblical calendar, the year "1994" actually lasted through March 1995, so humanity had six more months to repent, and prepare for the return of Christ and the end of the world. March 31st, he said, was probably the new target date, although even then he admitted to *San Francisco Chronicle* reporter Don Lattin, "You know, I'm like the boy who cried wolf again and again and the wolf didn't come. This doesn't bother me in the slightest."

> *"I'm like the boy who cried wolf again and again and the wolf didn't come."*

It did, however, bother more orthodox Christian leaders. With Family Radio reaching a worldwide audience, many Christian pastors and evangelists spoke out against the Alamedan prophet of doom, saying that his broadcasts not only badly misrepresented Christian theology and Biblical interpretation to a huge audience, but instilled in listeners a dangerous fatalism and fanaticism. One Christian critic claimed that Family Radio had a monopoly on the religious airwaves in rapidly-Christianizing Nigeria, and that Chinese authorities had banned all End-Times teachings because of a panic caused by Camping's Asian broadcasts.

There was trouble within Camping's organization as well. After September 1994, one of his sons-in-law quit his job at Family Radio, reportedly embarrassed by the broadcasts. Another former employee told Don Lattin that donations to the Alameda ministry had dropped off dramatically since September 1994, and that Camping had his increasingly-disgruntled network's employees "over a barrel. He pays their paychecks, so they can't oppose him…. Now everyone is waiting to see what will happen March 31 [1995]."

Of course, nothing even marginally apocalyptic happened that day. So the radio-preacher did some more conceptual and semantic shuffling, and now claimed that the September 1994-March 1995 period was not the time of Rapture and Judgement Day, but of the Great Tribulation—the necessary period of chastisement that would precede the Last Days. He admitted that he hadn't quite worked out all the prophecies and dates, but that he was sure just a bit more reverse-engineering of Scripture would tease out the true, certain, final date of Doomsday.

In the wake of the failed prophecies, many listeners abandoned Camping and Family Radio. But he pressed on, and slowly rebuilt Family Radio's worldwide audience, convincing new listeners across the globe who hadn't heard of the 1994/95 debacle that he spoke with authority on matters Scriptural. By the 21st Century, Family Radio owned 55 stations in the United States, and was heard on scores more across the globe, with an estimated listenership in the millions.

Camping's book Time Has an End *predicted the world would end on May 21st, 2011.*

Doomsday in May

Around 2005, Camping found a critical new wrinkle in his complex, numerological Biblical interpretation. He told his radio and prayer-group listeners that he'd determined that 7,000 years had to pass after the Biblical Flood before the Apocalypse could happen. Since he'd fixed the year of the Flood at 4990 BC, the Year of Doom would be 2011. As for the exact date, Camping crunched some more Scriptural numbers, and determined that all true believers would be raptured into Heaven on May 21, 2011.

To publicize his claims beyond Family Radio's airwaves, Camping produced a new book, *Time Has an End*. The book reworked and updated many of the earlier themes of 1994? tracing the history of the world along Camping's Biblical timeline and selecting carefully-interpreted Scriptural chapter and verse to bolster his claims that May 21, 2011 would see the Rapture of true Christians into Heaven, immediately followed by worldwide disasters that would annihilate civilization, and bring mass chaos and death across the planet.

> *"Beyond the shadow of a doubt, May 21 will be the date of the Rapture and the day of judgment."*

Camping's vision of 5/21/2011 was dire indeed. At precisely 6 p.m. that day, he said, deep beneath the Pacific Ocean, two tectonic plates would shift violently and create a cataclysmic worldwide earthquake whose massive shockwaves would roll eastward, flattening the world's great cities. Towering tsunamis, erupting volcanoes, exploding nuclear reactors, and airplanes falling from the sky would follow the temblor, destroying everything in their path. And through the tumult, a single trumpet would sound from Heaven as 100 million-odd true, Bible-/Camping-believing Christians were bodily lifted into Heaven, leaving behind six billion-plus heretics, heathens, and scoffers to suffer, and cry to the Lord for mercy and deliverance.

Over the next six years, Camping, his employees, and his followers raised an estimated $100 million to finance one of the greatest Christian media-blitzes in history. Family Radio erected 5,000 billboards across the United States and 30 other nations emblazoned with "Judgment Day: May 21" in huge letters, below which was the station's Web address. On its Web site, as well as over its worldwide radio network, Camping's Bible instruction was broadcast 24 hours a day, in 75 languages. And the radio-ministry freely distributed millions of copies of *Time Has an End* and other works that documented Camping's Doomsday predictions.

By early 2011, The New York Times, the BBC, and al-Jazeera, along with thousands of other newspapers, radio and TV stations, and Internet news feeds, were featuring stories on Family Radio's global-apocalypse saturation campaign, and the 89 year-old evangelist who was dead certain that May 21st would mark the Rapture. Journalists from across the globe converged on Family Radio's modest Alameda studios to interview the 21st-century prophet of doom, and puzzle over his complex calculations of coded Bible secrets. In photos and video-clips, the gaunt, lantern-jawed, cheap suit-clad Camping looked every bit a half-crazed street-corner evangelist now thrust in front of a worldwide audience.

Camping was absolutely sure that this time he had fixed the true timetable for the End Times. "Beyond the shadow of a doubt, May 21 will be the date of the Rapture and the day of judgment," he told an Associated Press reporter. The journalist noted that both individuals and independent Christian fellowships had picked up on Camping's message, and were

Billboards like these appeared all over the world in early 2011.

traveling across the globe in vehicles festooned with Biblical quotes about the Last Days, passing out Family Radio literature and warning all and sundry that the End was fast approaching.

*Camping's **fourth** precise prediction of Doomsday was virtually unprecedented in American religious history.*

Reactions to Camping's hugely-publicized prophecy among established Christian churches ranged from cautious skepticism, to embarrassment, to alarm and outraged calumny. Although theologians and Bible scholars pointed out the mistakes and improbabilities in Camping's interpretations and timeline, and although church pastors pleaded with their flocks to not heed the words of the Alamedan Cassandra, countless Christians across the globe stayed tuned to Family Radio, and prepared for a May 21st Rapture.

Atheists and skeptics had a field day with Camping and Family Radio. To many unbelievers, the Alamedan's doomsday rhetoric perfectly distilled what they saw as the delusion, paranoia, and sheer meanness of "Bible-believing" Christianity, and secularist individuals and groups lambasted and lampooned Camping with a vengeance, urging the public to ignore not only the radio preacher, but all self-proclaimed spokespeople of God and their irrational and absurd promises and threats.

As May 21st approached, news outlets reported that some Camping faithful had quit their jobs, maxed out credit-cards, eloped, or donated six-figure fortunes to the radio station, all anticipating their physical ascension into Heaven just days away. Darker stories told of people across the globe who committed suicide or murdered loved ones, rather than face the horrors of Doomsday. Although the murder/suicide reports later turned out to be unrelated to the chiliastic fervor, there was no mistaking the fact that Camping's prognostication was becoming one of the big news stories of the year.

On Friday, May 19th, Camping gave what would ostensibly be his final "Open Forum" broadcast ever. During the 90-minute program, he fielded calls from faithful listeners wishing him—and the world—goodbye, as well as jeers from naysayers. After the program concluded, he said goodbye to his Family Radio coworkers, closed the offices, and took his wife Shirley to a hotel, where they would spend the next 48 hours watching television news reports, and praying.

Finally, the day Camping, his countless followers, and the merely curious had been long anticipating, arrived. Sunday May 21st dawned on the East side of the International Date Line, and as clocks in the Western Pacific time zones counted off the minutes until 1800 hours—the precise moment of the first Rapture wave, according to Camping—Family Radio devotees across the world sang, prayed, and monitored TV and Internet news for confirmation that The End was here.

> *"The end is going to come very, very quietly."*

But The End never arrived.

The Fourth Strike

If anyone had expected Camping to shame-facedly abandon the airwaves and fade into obscurity after May 21st, they were to be disappointed. After telling reporters he was "flabbergasted" by the non-event, Camping immediately returned to his on-air post on Family Radio the following day, in the wake of what seemed to be the most publicized Doomsday prophecy in history.

That day, and for weeks afterwards, Camping followers, non-affiliated Christians, and skeptics alike bombarded "Open Forum"'s phone lines, calling the Alamedan a false prophet and rebuking him for misleading and terrifying people across the globe. Some individuals and groups filed petitions to have the stations' FCC license revoked, and more than one caller demanded he refund donors the millions he'd taken to publicize his less-than-accurate prognostications. The *Christian Post* even suggested that Camping had incurred God's wrath for misleading his listeners, and might be damned for his works.

On the airwaves Camping insisted that the Earth did in fact tremble with God's wrath on May 21st, since humans, formed of the planet's dust, had most certainly shaken, rattled, and rolled *en masse* in the face of his doomsday proclamation. May 21st, Camping said, had been an "invisible judgment day" when God had determined who truly believed the End was nigh; those who had ignored or scoffed at the prophecy were now under the Lord's judgment. He predicted the *physical* Judgment Day would arrive in less than five months, on October 21st.

Camping's *fourth* precise prediction of Doomsday was virtually unprecedented in American religious history. Even the fanatical followers of Massachusetts Baptist preacher William Miller, who had used similarly arcane methods of Bible interpretation to predict the end of the world, had given up after his third failed prophecy in 1844, and settled down to become what we now know as Adventists.

New York magazine reporter Dan Lee marveled at the fact that, weeks after May 21st, dozens of Campingites still met every Sunday at the Alameda Veteran's Building, holding low-key services and praying for the souls of their unsaved, unbelieving families and friends who were due to be annihilated in late October. Yet Lee also noted that many of the faithful seemed to be merely going through the motions of devotion, and detected traces of self-conscious embarrassment and doubt among Camping's followers, fellow Family Radio employees, and family alike. The network itself cancelled "Open Forum" that June 23rd, ending Camping's 50-year radio career.

In the weeks before October 21st, a stroke-afflicted, ailing Camping kept in touch with the faithful via recorded messages and podcasts. Observers noted that the Alamedan's prophecies of doom now used words like "maybe" and "probably" when he spoke of what would happen on the date, and that he soft-pedaled warnings of earthly disaster, saying "there's going to be no big display of any kind. The end is going to come very, very quietly."

But once again, the End never came. For the fourth consecutive time, Camping had struck out, and his remaining followers scattered. Chastened, he retreated from public view.

By March 2012, Camping was openly conceding failure. "We realize that many people are hoping they will know the date of Christ's return," he wrote in a letter to Family Radio listeners. "God has humbled us through the events of May 21… We must also openly acknowledge that we have no new evidence pointing to another date for the end of the world."

Camping's own End Times arrived quietly on December 15, 2013. That day Family Radio announced that the 92 year-old radio preacher and sometime Prophet of Doom had passed on from complications of a fall he had sustained two weeks earlier. The network survived him, and continues to broadcast Evangelical programs across the world's airwaves.

No doubt there will be more harbingers of doomsday to come. The fear of a great, final annihilation, and the hope of being swept away to a greater life, are as old as the human race itself. Clever, charismatic prophets of End Times like Alameda's Harold Camping will continue to find eager audiences as long as human beings, weary of their broken planet and sinful species, seek supernatural delivery from the drudgery and boredom of daily life.

13
David "Moses" Berg
& the Children of God

On January 8th, 2005, a grisly murder-suicide put the California-born Children of God back in the headlines. That evening, Ricky "Davidito" Rodriguez, the sect's 29 year-old "Divine Prince" and heir apparent, stabbed his former nanny, sect member Angela Smith, to death in his Tucson, Arizona apartment. Then he drove west to the desert town of Blythe, California, where he blew his brains out with a Glock pistol.

Ricky left behind a wife, a half-sister, and a circle of fellow "survivors," as well as a series of Internet postings and a video that described the sexual abuse he suffered in the Children of God—a secretive Christian sect that once promoted open, "liberated" eroticism, even for small children, and is still regarded by many as a destructive cult.

A Revolution for Jesus

The sect was in many ways the fruit of Christian evangelist's David Brandt Berg's childhood traumas. Later known to his followers as Moses or "Mo," Berg was born in 1919, the son of Miami-based revivalist Virginia Brandt Berg, who toured

David "Moses" Berg
with Davidito

Berg was a self-proclaimed Prophet, preaching a "Gospel of rebellion" and a "Revolution for Jesus."

America with her husband Hjalmer as the "Berg Evangelistic Drama Company."

Berg was haunted by childhood memories of sexual repression and frustration. He recalled that his mother once caught him masturbating, grabbed a knife, and threatened to emasculate him if he continued. He also said that his babysitter would fellate him to sleep every afternoon until one day when Mama Berg intervened, and threw her out of the house. And he remembered one night in his teens when, during a California trip, he'd shared a bed with his mother, and got an erection when her body pressed against his.

In 1941, the 22 year-old Berg was ordained to the Christian and Missionary Alliance. Four years later, after serving in the Army Corps of Engineers, he met Jane Miller at an Alliance Church in Van Nuys, California; they married shortly thereafter, and eventually produced four children.

Berg moved his family to the Alliance's Valley Farms settlement in Arizona, where he found work as a pastor. However, in 1951 he was caught having an affair with a 17-year old girl there, and left the community.

Berg soon found a new job in Texas with Fred Jordan, one of the first televangelists, and worked with him for the next sixteen years. His eldest daughter Deborah later claimed that during this period, he tried to molest her several times, and had also started an incestuous relationship with her younger sister Faithy.

Fired by Jordan in 1967, Berg and his family retreated to Huntington Beach, California, where his mother was living. Although retired, the elderly Virginia Berg had continued her evangelical work—this time informally—among the long-haired, scruffily-dressed young people who hung out along the beach boardwalk and pier. Her son, a suit-clad "square," joined her on her missions to the beach town's hippies and runaways.

After Berg's mother passed away, he took over her Huntington Beach ministry, and opened up a Christian youth center called the Light Club. Every night young seekers gathered at the funky storefront chapel to listen to Berg, who'd shed his three-piece suit for jeans and a work shirt, and had grown long hair and a beard.

In his sermons, the graying, 50 year-old father of four lambasted the "System": the older generation, and the established churches, government, capitalist economy, and military that served their corrupt, worldly interests. Berg had rejected the role of mere Christian pastor—now he was a self-proclaimed Prophet, preaching a "Gospel of rebellion" and a "Revolution for Jesus."

In the spirit of the times, Berg and his flock took their message to the streets. Clad in dark robes, they demonstrated at mainstream churches throughout the Southland, accusing the established sects of heresy. Their antics angered local officials and "System" churches, and fearing persecution, Berg and a few dozen faithful fled to Tucson, Arizona in 1969.

Prophet of Doom

One of his closest Tucson followers was 22 year-old Karen Zerby. There, Berg took her as his lover, and justified it as a polygamous arrangement permitted for God's true prophets, with his legal wife Jane as "Old Church," and young Karen—who was now calling herself "Maria"— as "New Church." The explanation satisfied both his followers and his wife, and Karen/Maria herself remained Berg's common-law spouse for the rest of his life.

As the Seventies dawned, Berg went into *Prophet of Doom* mode, telling both his followers and reporters that a devastating earthquake would push California into the ocean, that Europe and North America would incinerate each other in a massive nuclear war, and that the youth of the world had to repent and save their souls from the older generation's Antichrist System.

His followers appeared at demonstrations and government offices, wearing sackcloth, sporting wooden staves and ash-stained foreheads, and preaching their leader's apocalyptic creed. Thousands of youths, fearing for the future and disillusioned with the increasingly cynical and drug-sodden counterculture, joined them. When a group of these Christian hippies told a New Jersey reporter that they "were not part of any church or group, just Children of God," the name stuck, and became the sect's formal title for years thereafter.

Berg housed and trained many of his followers at Fred Jordan's abandoned 400-acre ranch, as well as at a network of Christian communes across the West. Hundreds of drug casualties, runaways, and other young misfits were bused into these settlements by Children of God evangelists, and turned all their worldly goods over to the group to help finance the sect's now-global crusade. Others formed communes and roving gypsy bands across North America and Europe.

Berg ran the movement via *The Mo Letters*: a series of hundreds of essays, instruction booklets, and rants he wrote over a 25-year period to educate and enlighten his followers. The *Mo Letters* included such peculiar pieces as "I Am a Toilet—Are You?" a 1972 homily where Berg turned the act of defecation into a metaphor for Christian salvation, and urged the reader to become a fellow "Toilet for Jesus." Others were less humorous, such as his anti-Semitic screeds that called the Jewish people "antichrist," praised Hitler for attempting to check their power, and claimed that the Holocaust was a hoax designed to guilt-trip Christians.

Berg's militant rhetoric, and the Children's rejection of mainstream Western life, alarmed many members' parents. San Diegan Ted Patrick became convinced Berg was brainwashing his followers, and invented the hugely-controversial process of "cult deprogramming," where he and his associates waylaid members of the Children and other offbeat sects, held them in seclusion, and tried to erase whatever indoctrination they'd received. Though many criticized Patrick's tactics, they also conceded that David Berg looked less like a modern-day Moses, and more like a Pied Piper leading American children into physical, mental, and spiritual slavery.

"I Am a Toilet— Are You?"

Hookers for Jesus

And the controversies were only beginning. In early 1974, Berg started teaching what he called "The Law of Love": a doctrine that said the Children were "God's last church" and that, so long as one's actions were motivated solely by love for God and others, all Biblical legal restrictions were null and void—especially those pertaining to sex. One 1977 tract, "Love vs. Law!" proclaimed, "As far as the Bible says, for us there is no such thing as adultery!"

Berg put this libidinous doctrine into practice with a novel evangelical technique that would be forever identified with his sect. The patriarch told his female disciples that it was now their duty to become "heaven's harlots," and sacrifice their bodies for Christ, that they might bring men into the Church.

Berg instructed his "girls" on how to turn a simple one-night-stand into a loving welcome into the Christian faith. He ordered his "hookers for Jesus" to perform "masturbation, sucking and actual intercourse…It's all, or nothing at all! Halle-lujah!" Berg even advised his female missionaries to endure rape as one might tolerate the greed of a starving child, and speculated that forced gang-bangs could be an excellent opportunity to witness for the Lord.

The sexual-missionary practice would be dubbed "flirty fishing," or FF'ing, after Christ's declaration in *Matthew 4:19,* "Follow me, and I will make you fishers of men." Berg would issue many *Mo Letters* on the theory and practice of this Christian sacred-whoredom, such as "The Little Flirty Fishy," a children's comic book that explained the practice to Berg's preteen followers.

*A Mo Letter **advocating sexual seduction for Christ***

Berg's entourage of Flirty Fishers followed him to Spain's Canary Islands in 1974, where both female and male Children turned their evangelical and erotic attentions to the region's many tourists. Shortly thereafter, both *Time* and *Stern* magazines published pieces on Berg, his followers, and their paradoxical melding of Christian witness with

Swinging-Seventies sexuality. When the Canarian Catholic hierarchy caught wind of the sect and complained to officials, Berg fled to mainland Europe, where his followers now numbered in the thousands and had established colonies in six countries.

Since the name "Children of God" had become synonymous with both spiritual and sexual cultism in much of the media, Berg renamed his movement "The Family of Love," or more simply, "The Family." He also centralized the sect, ousting his regional lieutenants and organizing the Family as a network of cells that answered directly to him. Berg urged members to either go underground and stay on the move from the System, or infiltrate mainstream Christian churches and inject his teachings into their practices. And he refocused the group's missionary efforts on the Third World, where the System's media and churches held less sway, and the suffering masses yearned for delivery from oppression.

> "[M]asturbation, sucking and actual intercourse…It's all, or nothing at all! Hallelujah!"

The transformation of the Family into a global spiritual guerrilla movement, as well as the increasing emphasis on sexuality and separation from "the world," cost Berg thousands of followers. Those who remained were wholly committed to his vision of erotic evangelism and Christian world revolution, and although the group became less visible, its practices were more radical than ever.

Davidito

No person more symbolized the ideals of Berg and the Family than Richard Peter "Ricky" Rodriguez, the son of Karen-Maria Zerby and a Canarian hotel worker whom she'd "flirty-fished." Berg, who'd arranged the coupling, christened the boy *Davidito* and proclaimed that he and his mother were the "Two Witnesses" mentioned in *Revelation 11* that would usher in the Apocalypse. The aging patriarch raised little Ricky/Davidito as both his own son and his ostensible heir to the throne—a Divine Prince who would be a living symbol of the Family's commitment to create a new kind of Christian.

The Story of Davidito contained photos of Ricky in sex play with both his nannies and other children.

As a religious patriarch living in a private cell of compliant young females, Berg indulged his sexual-liberation ideals fully in Ricky's raising. The boy's early years were documented in a 1982 Family-published book called *The Story of Davidito* that was distributed to Family enclaves around the world, and offered as a guide to raising the sect's children free of sexual shame and guilt.

The Story of Davidito was filled with anecdotes and pictures of Ricky in sex play with both his nannies and other Family children, including one photo that depicted an adult female sucking the toddler's penis. The adults' identities were disguised with cartoon-like faces that had been drawn over their real likenesses, largely to protect Berg and his associates, who were often on the run from government authorities.

But Ricky wasn't Berg's only young victim. Berg also continually molested Ricky's half-sister Davida, and his granddaughter Merry. When Merry disobeyed Berg's orders to sleep with Ricky and produce a child, the patriarch tied her to her bed, beat her with a rod, spanked her bare bottom in front of her friends and Family adults, and published the account of the "exorcism" in a *Mo Letter* called "The Last State."

Within Family colonies, Berg set up groups known as "Teen Combos" to indoctrinate, educate, and socialize adolescents, and crush any rebellion they might display towards him, the sect, or their way of life. Troublemaking teens were sent to so-called "Victory Camps" where they

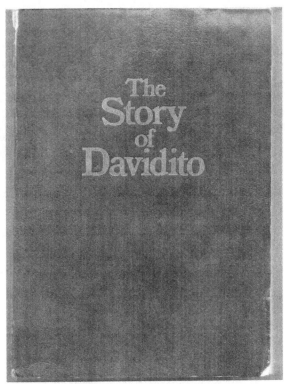

The Story of Davidito

were kept in isolation, and subject to Berg's arbitrary and ever-changing rules on behavior and discipline. Reports of beatings and sexual abuse at the camps began to filter through the close-knit world of the Family.

In the late 1980s, Berg ran the camps, as well as the rest of the sect, from "The Heavenly City"—a secretive Family settlement in Japan that also housed Ricky and the rest of Berg's entourage. Initiated into full sexual intercourse at age 12, Ricky spent his teens living out Berg's ideal of sexual freedom, copulating with both other adolescents and adults, including—according to Davida—his own mother. Although Ricky later vehemently denied he had an Oedipal relationship with Karen/Maria, he testified in detail about the orgiastic goings-on at Family compounds, where mate-swapping and group sex-parties were regular events.

Former Family child River Phoenix once claimed he lost his virginity at the age of four.

"We Shall Have a Great, Big Orgy Together!"

By the early 1990s, the Family was once again generating media interest—most of it highly negative. Now an adult, Merry Berg went on NBC TV's "Now" news show in September 1993, and discussed her sexual and physical abuse at the hands of Berg and other Family elders. Soon afterwards, she and other Family children testified in a high-profile British child-custody case involving the Family that exposed much of their hyper-sexualized culture to public view. And on Halloween 1993, film star and Family child River Phoenix, who once claimed he lost his virginity at the age of four, died in a Hollywood gutter of a drug overdose—hardly a fitting tribute to Berg's idealization of childhood sexuality.

Along with the personal revelations, documented evidence of the Family's sexual shenanigans surfaced as well. Part of *The Story of Davidito* was leaked to the press, and one Family defector turned over sixteen trunks' worth of pilfered top-secret Family sex videos and literature to reporters.

In response, the Family commissioned an independent study of Ricky and other Family kids that concluded there was no hard evidence of maladjustment or molestation among them. They also pointed out that despite all the seeming evidence against them, nobody in the group had ever been convicted of any crimes against children. And they claimed that they'd renounced their more extreme doctrines about childhood sex, and had abandoned flirty-fishing in 1987 when AIDS made the practice too dangerous.

When the 75 year-old Berg passed on in 1994, Karen/Maria immediately took over the reins of leadership. She soon introduced a teaching called "Marriage of the Generations," where young-adult Family faithful were encouraged to sleep with much-older members, in order to promote harmony and unity in the sect. One of her "prophecies," "Loving Jesus!" had Christ Himself urging Family members to masturbate while praying to him, saying, "We shall have a great feast and we shall have great love, and we shall have a great, great, great big orgy together!" To critics of the Family, as well as disgruntled defectors, it seemed as if the sect was just recreating the erotic-evangelism environment that had caused all the past trouble and tragedy.

In 2000, Ricky/Davidito Rodriguez, now 25 and married to a Family member named Elixcia, publically denounced and quit the sect. Over the next four years he wrote many Internet postings about his bizarre childhood, and the deep and painful psychic wounds he'd endured from it.

Although Ricky and his wife tried to settle into a "normal" life in Washington State, the past had far too strong a hold on him. As he put it in a 2004 post on an anti-Family Internet site:

I was under the mistaken impression that having written [about my story] I could leave it all behind, start a new life that had nothing to do with the cult, and really 'move on' with my life. I know now that will never happen. I can't run away from my past... Something has to be done to stop these child molesters...Every day these people [who] are alive and free [are] a slap in the face to the thousands of us who've been methodically molested, tortured, raped, and the many who they have as good as murdered by driving them to suicide.

"Something has to be done to stop these child molesters…"

Ricky was obsessed with finding his mother, Karen/Maria. In September 2004 he moved to Tucson, Arizona, thinking that the peripatetic Family leader might land in her old hometown to visit her sister Rosemary. Ominously, he started speaking and writing about killing the Family Queen, and backed up his threats by purchasing a Glock pistol.

Murder in Tucson, Suicide in Blythe

Finally, on January 7, 2005, he made a rambling confessional video of himself in his kitchen, recounting his sufferings at the hands of the Family, and wavering between thoughts of suicide, threats of vengeance, and doubts that he could carry out either path of action. The next day he got in touch with Sue Kauten AKA Angela Smith, a close associate of his mother's and one of the first flirty-fishers.

An old nanny of Ricky's, who appeared in *Story of Davidito* photos playing sex games with the little boy, the 51-year old Kauten/Smith met Ricky at his Tucson apartment on the evening of January 8th, but never left it alive. The coroner's report on her death determined that Ricky killed her with a single knife wound to her neck.

While Kauten/Smith's corpse was still warm, Ricky jumped into his car, and drove west. Several hours later, after he called his wife and confessed the murder, he turned onto a dirt access road south of Blythe, California, parked the car, and blew his brains out. His bullet-shattered corpse was found the next morning by an irrigation worker.

The murder-suicide once again put the Family in the national news, and brought home the reality and tragedy of the sect's excesses and abuses. Although some speculated that Ricky had driven to California to hunt his mother and other sect leaders, only to lose his nerve in Blythe, most observers felt that Ricky had given up on life completely, and had killed Kauten/Smith as a last symbolic, bloody gesture to the Family before he sent a bullet through his own skull.

Ricky killed his old nanny with a single knife wound to the neck.

As with all the other scandals that beset it, the Family weathered the Ricky Rodriguez suicide-murder. Today, if one peruses its slickly-designed Web site, it seems to be just another evangelical Christian organization spreading the Good News and doing humanitarian work across the globe. But its critics and "survivors" maintain that it has never officially repudiated Berg's doctrines, and that it continues to preach and practice in his spirit, often behind the cover of front groups. The Family remains controversial and the subject of investigations and exposes by both journalists and various national governments.

Ricky Rodriguez, hours before the murder-suicide

The seeds that were planted on the Huntington Beach boardwalk over forty years ago have long since brought forth creeping tendrils that have circled the world, sometimes entangling young and innocent victims in its vines. Whether the Family is an innocent—if strange—growth, or a noxious weed, will ultimately be determined by the Harvester that David Berg claimed to represent during his time as a modern-day Prophet and Patriarch of the world's alienated youth.

The Jesus Freaks

David Berg wasn't the only evangelist who reached out to the California Sixties counterculture. Three hundred miles north of Huntington Beach, in San Francisco's Haight-Ashbury district, converted hippies in the "Living Room" mission witnessed to young people who'd been alienated from both mainstream America and the various come-ons of the "alternative culture."

Across the Bay, in radical Berkeley, Old-Time Religion met the New Left as Jack Sparks' Christian World Liberation Front preached an activist Gospel that recast the Prince of Peace as a Che Guevara-esque revolutionary whose teachings opposed the violence and decadence of a corrupt empire, and who would lead oppressed peoples to freedom and equality.

Ronald Enroth's 1972 study of "The Jesus People"

All over California—and soon, America—Christian communes formed, likening themselves to the original cells of believers in first-Century Rome. The so-called "Jesus Revolution" was underway, and its followers would be called "Jesus people," or more derisively, "Jesus Freaks."

Perhaps the most flamboyant of California's "Jesus Freaks" was West Hollywood's Arthur Blessitt. The Mississippi-born Blessitt began his evangelical career in 1968 as "The Minister of the Sunset Strip," witnessing to the hippies, bikers, runaways, prostitutes, and other lost souls who visited his Christian coffee-house, *His Place*, situated next door to a topless-club. The coffee-house sported a large wooden cross that Blessitt eventually carried on a never-ending worldwide pilgrimage to war-torn and poverty-stricken places across the globe; to date, he's borne the cross nearly 20,000 miles through nearly every nation on Earth, and has been the subject of several documentaries that examine his unique, back-breaking personal crusade.

For the most part, California's countercultural Christians have identified not with the faith's liberal or mystical tendencies, but with the evangelical, fundamentalist strain of American Christianity that stressed the "born-again" experience, literal Biblical interpretation, and apocalyptic "end-times" theology. Like the hippies themselves, this form of Christianity had been largely a mocked, marginalized subculture in secularizing, sophisticated postwar America, until its earthy, emotive spirituality was rediscovered by a generation of young people seeking authenticity and truth. Though few would admit it today, much of American Fundamentalist Christianity's post-Sixties cultural and political power was forged in this unlikely alliance between youth rebellion and religious traditionalism.

14

Troy Perry
& the Metropolitan Community Church

No Christian movement in California—and few in American history—has endured as much persecution and terrorism since its founding as Los Angeles' Metropolitan Community Church, or had quite as much impact on the nation's sexual mores and attitudes.

Rev. Troy Perry in 2006

Jonathunder

In the wake of the Sixties' Civil Rights Movement, where Southern Black churches were torched and bombed by racist terrorists, the MCC took up a far more controversial cause, and served a much less "visible" minority group, in the name of Christian love and social justice. Its primary—but not exclusive—ministry was to a population that had been condemned, disparaged, marginalized, imprisoned, tortured, and murdered throughout twenty-five centuries of Judeo-Christian history: homosexuals.

The Spirit and the Flesh

The Metropolitan Community Church grew out of the ministry of Reverend Troy D. Perry. Raised a Southern

Baptist in Florida, Perry ran away from home at twelve after being beaten repeatedly by his drunken stepfather, and raped by a family friend. He sought sanctuary with his Pentecostal relatives, whose emotional, passionate worship style spoke to the adolescent's pains and hopes.

Perry was terrified that God would strike him dead for drinking his first beer.

Perry returned home with the Pentecostal spirit, dropped out of high school at sixteen, and became a paid Church of God evangelist in Alabama. He also discreetly explored his budding homosexuality with several local men, but suppressed it when a Church minister told him the love of a good woman would cure him of same-sex desire.

So, at eighteen Perry married the minister's daughter, and moved to Joliet, Illinois, where he found work, attended a Bible college, and pastored a small Church of God congregation. But a Church elder found out about the young minister's gay dalliances back in Alabama, and quietly removed him from the pulpit.

Still on fire for the Lord, Perry joined the rival Church of God of Prophecy, and moved to Torrance, California, far from the scandals dogging his ministry. Although he pastored a thriving congregation in the Los Angeles suburb, he grew disenchanted with the Church's strait-laced strictures. And his marriage, although it had produced two sons, was loveless.

When Perry read Donald Webster Cory's classic study, *The Homosexual in America*, he realized he would never be "cured" of his inclinations, and he couldn't live in the closet anymore. Perry "came out" to both his wife and his ecclesiastical superior with predictable results: he was divorced, and excommunicated.

Freed from both familial and ministerial obligations, the 22-year-old Southern Pentecostal preacher took his first tentative steps into the early-1960s L.A. gay underground. In his memoir *Don't Be Afraid Anymore*, Perry recounted his maiden visit to a gay bar, where he was terrified that God would strike him dead on the spot for drinking his first beer!

Two years later, Perry was drafted into the U.S. Army. He served three years as a teletype operator in West Germany, and upon his discharge in 1967, he returned to Los Angeles, where he found a job, roomed with an old friend, and dove back into the Southern California gay scene.

A Church for People in Trouble

In that pre-Stonewall period, Southland gays mostly gathered in small, scattered bars, under constant siege from both vice cops and queer-bashing thugs. When his friend Tony was busted at one and threatened with exposure, Perry suggested he pray for strength and guidance, only to be rebuffed by the self-loathing "dirty queer," who'd been excommunicated from the Catholic Church for his homosexuality, and couldn't conceive of a God who would accept him.

"We need… a special church that will reach out to the lesbian and gay community."

Distraught, Perry prayed for a church that would recognize that gays and lesbians were God's children, and deserving of His love as much as heterosexuals. "Lord, you called me to preach," he recounted praying in his memoir. "We need a church, not a homosexual church, but a special church that will reach out to the lesbian and gay community. A church for people in trouble, and for people who just want to be near you. So, if you want such a church started, and you seem to keep telling me that you do, well then, just let me know when."

And a still, small voice said to the gay Pentecostal preacher, "Now."

For the next few weeks, Perry prepared to hold the first openly gay-friendly Christian church service in known history. He picked the name "Metropolitan Community Church" for his group, then spread word among his friends, and took out an ad in *The Advocate*, L.A.'s gay-oriented newspaper. Perry readied the front room of his Huntington Park home as a chapel, and a sympathetic Congregationalist minister loaned him a clerical robe, hymnals, and communion bread.

On the afternoon of October 6, 1968, Perry and twelve worshippers gathered in his living room for the Metropolitan Community Church's first service. Clad in liturgical robes for the first time in his clerical career, the erstwhile-Pentecostal Perry conducted a low-key service with prayers, a homily, and an LP of traditional hymns playing in the background.

Jesus, Perry said, spoke against lust—the sin of using people for sexual gratification, rather than the loving communion of sex, straight or gay.

Reverend Perry's sermon that first Sunday was titled, "Be True to You." It outlined his threefold vision of the Church's ministry: 1) *Salvation*, through the love of Christ, which did not exclude gays; 2) *Community*, for a sacred family of faithful Christians rejected by the religious Establishment; and 3) *Christian Social Action*, to fight the oppression and injustice that plagued homosexuals. All three concepts would define the Church's mission in the coming years.

By the end of 1968, Perry's home could no longer contain the growing flock of Sunday worshippers. So the Church rented Hollywood's Encore Theater for gatherings, and every Sunday through the end of 1970, nearly 200 gay men, along with a goodly number of lesbians and heterosexuals, filled its seats for worship services.

WE HAVE 1000 SEATS TO FILL!

FOR

"SPIRITUAL RENEWAL DAY '70"

Hear the Homosexual Community's own REVEREND TROY D. PERRY

Sunday September 13 7:00 P.M. at California Hall
Corner of Turk & Polk San Francisco

BE ONE OF THE 1000!
Sponsored by Metropolitan Community Church

A 1970 flyer for the MCC in San Francisco.

The "Sin of Sodom"

Perry knew that he and his flock were challenging one of the oldest and most ingrained prohibitions in the Christian tradition. Aware of the Bible chapters and verses cited as justifications for condemning gays, he spent much of his ensuing career challenging orthodox interpretations of them.

When critics invoked the story of Sodom and Gomorrah as an example of Biblical injunctions against homosexuality, Perry answered that both Scripture—such as *Ezekiel*

"God... cure the Episcopal bishop of his homophobia."

16: 48-50—and modern scholarship implied that hostility to strangers, rather than same-sex relations, was the "sin of Sodom" that brought God's fiery wrath down upon the "cities of the plain." When they cited verses in *Leviticus* that called same-sex relations an "abomination," Perry replied that they, like the prohibitions on wearing garments of mixed materials, or eating shellfish or rare meat, were Hebraic "Old Covenant" laws that had been nullified by Christ's sacrifice on the Cross.

Perry would often go on to say that Christ Himself never explicitly condemned homosexuality—the sexual sinners He confronted, such as the woman at the well and the woman caught in adultery, were straight. Jesus, Perry said, spoke against lust—the sin of using people for sexual gratification, rather than sharing with them the loving communion of sex, straight or gay.

As for St. Paul's pronouncements against same-sex relations in *Romans, 1 Corinthians* and *1 Timothy,* Perry maintained that the Apostle's language was ambiguous, and that he was probably condemning ritual-sex with male temple-prostitutes, rather than simple homosexuality. Perry also pointed out that Paul peppered the Epistles with all sorts of statements—forbidding women to speak in church, condoning slavery—that had historically been used to justify oppression. For Perry, the time had come for Christendom to abandon gay-bashing in the name of God, much as previous generations of progressive Christians had rejected "Bible-justified" slavery, racism, and misogyny.

Perry and the MCC made national headlines in December 1970 when he attempted to perform a same-sex wedding at a rented Washington, D.C. Episcopal church. When the local Bishop got word that one of his parishes was going to be defiled by "perverts," he locked Perry and his sixteen followers out of the building, leaving them to perform simple nuptials and a communion service in the freezing snow. Perry then led his little band on an impromptu march to the National Cathedral, where he stood at the altar and preached a sermon asking for God "to cure the Episcopal bishop of his homophobia."

Radical Inclusion and Terror

The Metropolitan Community Church grew rapidly in the early Seventies, after the Stonewall riots and the general liberalizing of American society brought countless gay men, lesbians, bisexuals, and transsexuals out of the closet and into a conscious community. Perry traveled incessantly across America, planting new MCC congregations and networking with homosexual Christians, impressing both allies and opponents with his energy, charisma, and political moxie. By early 1971, the Los Angeles Mother Church was well-heeled and attended enough to purchase a permanent place of worship—an old church building at 22nd and Union, on the edge of the L.A. ghetto.

There, as well as at the many local groups he visited, the gay Reverend preached and practiced a Gospel of radical inclusion. The MCC admitted its first female minister, the Reverend Freda Smith, in 1972, and committed itself to gender equality and an increased ministry to the lesbian and "woman-identified" communities. Blind and deaf Christians were accommodated with Braille materials and sign-language interpreters. Some congregations even welcomed transsexuals and leather fetishists—then considered controversial in much of the gay world.

Despite its ultra-liberal stance in the fields of human sexuality and social action, the MCC always retained a fairly orthodox, Nicene-creed-influenced statement of faith as its primary *raison d'etre*. To Perry, the MCC was Christian first and gay-friendly second, although he did allow and approve of such innovations as witnessing in gay bars and nightclubs, having handholding couples take communion together, and sermons with humor and references drawn from, and directed to, the gay subculture.

As might have been expected, the backlash against the MCC was fierce. MCC pastors and faithful were verbally abused and physically assaulted in public, and MCC churches across America were picketed, vandalized, and even firebombed—including Los Angeles' "Mother Church," destroyed by a mysterious fire in 1973. Seventeen MCC meeting places were set aflame by persons unknown, and it wasn't until 1985 that bomb-threats ceased against the annual Church General Conference.

All these incidents paled in comparison to the New Orleans UpStairs fire. On June 24, 1973, an arsonist torched a French Quarter bar hosting a crowded MCC Gay-Pride party, killing 32 people– the deadliest conflagration in New Orleans history.

The local reaction was callous and insulting. Papers covering the story made snide insinuations about the UpStairs and its patrons, and published a macabre photo of MCC Rev. Bill Larson's charred corpse trapped in one of the UpStairs' windows. The city and state governments kept mum about the tragedy, save for the Police Chief of Detectives, who called the bar a hangout for "thieves" and "queers." And several bodies from the UpStairs were never claimed by their next of kin, too embarrassed to acknowledge that family members had died in a "queer bar."

Incensed, Perry and his associates traveled to New Orleans, demanding compassion for the dead, and respect for the gay community in the wake of the disaster. When they tried to organize a formal day of remembrance for the victims, they were barred from every religious building in New Orleans large enough to accommodate the hundreds of mourners who converged on the city.

Finally, when a small Methodist church agreed to hold a service for UpStairs victims, Perry alerted the national media, and news

A plaque memorializing 32 people who died in the UpStairs fire.

crews surrounded the building during the ceremony. Knowing that mourners would be photographed as soon as they stepped outside, Perry informed the assembled flock that the press was waiting for them, and gave attendees the option of exiting out a hidden back door. None took it.

Seventeen MCC meeting places were set aflame by persons unknown.

Activism and AIDS

The persecution of, and attendant publicity campaigns and activism by the MCC, prepared it to take a leading role in fighting larger-scale and legal—but equally dangerous—actions against the gay community. When California State Senator John Briggs sponsored a ballot initiative to ban gays from teaching in the state's schools, Perry organized fund-raising efforts and rallies to fight the measure. It was defeated soundly in the November 1978 election largely because of his work.

The Reverend Perry was becoming a major political player. In 1975 he spoke for gay rights at a meeting with Georgia's then-Governor Jimmy Carter; two years later, President Carter invited Perry to his inauguration, as well as to a White House meeting regarding the American gay political and cultural scene. Perry later remarked that his appearance on TV emerging from the White House not only helped bring countless gays and lesbians out of the closet, but also convinced his socially conservative relatives that if *Troy the Homosexual* was good enough to meet with the President, he was also good enough to be part of the family.

During the 1980s, Perry and the Church faced its greatest foe yet: the AIDS epidemic, which devastated the gay community, and eventually killed thousands of Church members. The MCC provided pastoral care and healing services for people afflicted with the disease, and successfully fought legal measures to quarantine or demonize AIDS victims and gays. And Perry and other gay theologians challenged the view that AIDS was God's punishment for sexual license, noting that nowhere in Scripture did Jesus threaten sinners with disease, and that the virus was nearly unknown among lesbians.

By the 21st Century, the Church called itself The Universal Fellowship of Metropolitan Community Churches, and claimed congregations in 45 U.S. States and in 23 nations. It was also granted Observer status in the World Council of Churches, further cementing its self-image as a mainstream, liberal-Christian denomination with a special ministry to an otherwise-neglected population.

And Perry's star continued to rise. During the Clinton Administration he was a guest at White House conferences on AIDS and hate crimes, as well as an attendee at a special Presidential breakfast for religious leaders. Perry also wrote two autobiographies, a collection of gay biographies, and a book of gay-themed Christian meditations, and contributed to several works on gay theology. The 65 year-old reverend retired from Church leadership in 2005, but he continued to speak before religious and political groups, and agitate for gay rights.

Leather-Bar Spirituality

Perry's life and work, as well as the history of the MCC, were the subjects of a 2007 documentary, *Call Me Troy*. Along with anecdotes and reminiscences about the Church and the rise of gay power and consciousness over the last four decades, the award-winning film featured a surprising revelation by the now grey-haired Reverend: he was a leather fetishist who regularly partied with gay-male sadomasochism enthusiasts.

The MCC actively ministers to transgendered people.

Perry told Canadian journalist Shaun Proulx that he was impressed by the "spirituality and the care—especially during AIDS—of leathermen, the owners of leather bars and clubs, just amazing…" The Reverend mentioned that, "Some of the things I've seen and witnessed at leather gatherings are akin to reading about the saints filled with rapture of being so involved with God and God's love," and viewed the S/M subculture as a powerful spiritual practice in its own right.

> *"Some of the things I've seen and witnessed at leather gatherings are akin to reading about the saints filled with rapture… "*

In the forty-plus years of the MCC's existence, Perry helped direct a massive change in both religious and social attitudes towards homosexuals, with many mainstream churches eventually soft-pedaling or even eliminating traditional condemnations of same-sex relationships, and forming "welcoming" programs for non-heterosexual seekers. Yet his Church remained as vibrant and healthy a sect as ever, offering gays and other "sexual minorities" a safe, supportive community where they could follow a Christian path without censure or judgment.

As with the original Christian church of 2,000 years earlier, a meeting of twelve people and their leader had led to a spiritual and social revolution. One can only speculate where the ripples radiating from that simple gathering in a Los Angeles living room will lead in the years to come.

Gay Hippie Evangelist

If Troy Perry is California's greatest openly-gay Christian evangelist, then Laguna Beach's Lonnie Frisbee might have been its most influential *closeted* one.

Like the MCC founder, Frisbee's Fifties childhood was marred by abuse, neglect, and rape. In his mid-teens he sought healing in art, and became an award-winning painter and dancer. He also regularly took LSD, and during one trip with friends in the mountains above Palm Springs, he was overwhelmed by the presence of Christ, and baptized his buddies in a nearby creek.

In 1967, Frisbee journeyed to San Francisco during the Summer of Love, lived in a Christian commune in the Haight-Ashbury, and hitchhiked California's roads, sharing the Gospel with hippies and "squares" alike. When he returned to Orange County in 1968, Frisbee joined evangelist Chuck Smith's Calvary Chapel, and won over the suit-clad Costa Mesan, who later said of the long-haired, bearded 19 year-old, "I was not at all prepared for the love that this young man would radiate."

During the late 1960s, Frisbee roamed the beaches from Costa Mesa to San Diego, witnessing to surfers and hippies, baptizing them *en masse* in the Pacific Ocean, and inviting them to services at Calvary Chapel. Handsome and charismatic, the young evangelist brought thousands of youth to Christ and the Chapel, and became one of the prime figures of the "Jesus Freaks" Christian-counterculture that spread from California across the globe.

Frisbee eventually split with Smith, but stayed friendly with Yorba Linda Calvary Chapel pastor Jon Wimber. When Wimber invited Frisbee to preach at his church, the charismatic evangelist called the Holy Spirit into the meet-

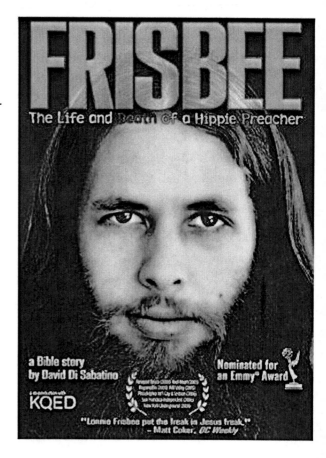

A 2005 documentary about Lonnie Frisbee.

ing, and the young people present fell to the floor and spoke in tongues much as the Azusa Revival (q.v.) faithful had done seventy years earlier. They took their "Spirit-baptized" fervor to the streets, and soon became known as the "Vineyard Movement"—a Christian renewal that rivaled the Calvary Chapel in its size and international scope.

Although he was said to perform healings and miracles wherever he went, Frisbee never resolved his own inner conflict between flesh and spirit. Actively homosexual since his mid-teens, the evangelist believed his same-sex desires were deeply sinful, yet indulged them regularly until he contracted AIDS in the late 1980s. Frisbee died in 1993, and was buried at the Crystal Cathedral Memorial Gardens in Garden Grove.

A 2005 Emmy-nominated documentary titled *Frisbee: The Life and Death of a Hippie Preacher* examined his life and work, and his posthumous memoir, *Not by Might, Nor by Power,* appeared seven years later. To this day, neither the Calvary Chapel nor the Vineyard Churches mention Frisbee in their Web sites or official literature.

15
Phil Aguilar
& the Set Free Ministry

Perhaps no single figure has polarized California's contemporary Evangelical Christian community as much as Anaheim's Phil Aguilar, a tattooed, reformed-addict, ex-felon biker who has ministered to alcoholics, junkies, gang members, homeless people, and others of the "least, last, and lost" for nearly forty years.

To his supporters, Aguilar is a fearless, passionate evangelist who's reached out to society's untouchables, and brought them out of the bondages of addiction, crime, and depravity, and into the love of Christ and a dynamic, supportive faith-community. To his detractors, he's an egomaniacal cult-guru who's abused his followers, bullied his critics, and exploited his ministry to build personal wealth and power.

A "Square Peg"

Aguilar himself concedes that he's a rebel and a "square peg." Growing up the only dark-skinned, Mexican-/American-Indian kid in his lily-white Fifties Anaheim neighborhood, he felt his outsider status from an early age. When his parents

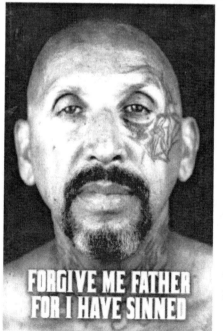

FORGIVE ME FATHER FOR I HAVE SINNED

Pastor Phil Aguilar's memoir

divorced in 1959, the 12 year-old Aguilar lost interest in school, and started drinking, smoking marijuana, and doing petty crimes.

Aguilar was dealing cocaine, and ended up with a ten-year prison sentence.

By his late teens Aguilar's rebellion had taken a different form. He grew his hair long, hung out with surfers, and dropped acid in the Southern California mountains with the Brotherhood of Eternal Love, an Orange County street-gang who'd renounced crime and violence for LSD and spirituality. He also dealt small amounts of pot—a pastime that led to an arrest, a year in jail, and his first up-close view of legal oppression and jailhouse brutality.

Upon his release in 1969, Aguilar toughened up, learning karate and becoming a professional black-belt master. He also married, and fathered a son named Geronimo, but the family broke up when Aguilar switched from pot and acid to cocaine and heroin, and sank into the depths of addiction. He also started dealing coke, and when he was tasked with delivering $100,000 worth of Peruvian flake, he instead got high on the supply, and went off on a violent, days-long drug-bender that ended with his arrest. Charged as a drug trafficker and domestic abuser, Aguilar got a ten-year sentence.

At Chino State Prison, Aguilar sobered up, married his girlfriend, and turned his life over to Christ. A model prisoner, he was released after serving just two years, and returned to Anaheim.

Set Free by Christ

Aguilar found work as a maintenance man, attended a Bible college, and eventually became an assistant pastor at an Anaheim Baptist church. But the denomination was too strait-laced and stodgy for the tattooed, Harley-riding ex-con who preferred leather jackets and rock n' roll to three-piece suits and traditional hymns. Aguilar sought to take his ministry into the streets, to bring the Good News to people like him who didn't fit the Baptist idea of what a Christian looked, talked, or dressed like.

In 1982 Aguilar founded Set Free Ministries, named after Jesus' promise in *John 8:32*, "Then you will know the truth, and the truth will set you free." With the blessing of Anaheim's then-Mayor Dan Roth, the Ministries set up shop in a large warehouse just down the street from City Hall.

The warehouse soon became a regional magnet for the junkies, drunks, homeless, ex-cons, gangbangers, outlaw-bikers, punks, *cholos*, and other social misfits attracted by Aguilar's message of unconditional love and healing from Christ. Set Free's T-shirted, jeans-wearing, gum-chewing flock enthused to the Anaheim native's energetic preaching, testified to their own sin-drenched pasts, and gave themselves to Christ at the altar, all to the soundtrack of the praise-chanting Christian punk and rap bands who played on the warehouse's low stage.

Junkies, drunks, punks, ex-cons, gangbangers, and other misfits came to worship at Set Free.

Aguilar also steered alcoholics, addicts, and homeless people to a network of private houses he'd rented around Anaheim, where they were sheltered, fed, and kept sober and busy by house overseers. The houses were open 24 hours a day to all comers, many of whom were "problem" types sent to Aguilar by other local churches not equipped to deal with their dysfunctions. One of the houses' highest-profile residents was Aguilar's oldest son Geronimo, who'd returned to him as a teenager and eventually became a junior Set Free pastor.

Aguilar's profile widened considerably when Jan and Paul Crouch of Costa Mesa's Trinity Broadcasting Network (TBN) offered him a Friday night TV show on their evangelical network. The pony-tailed, black-clad Latino pastor quickly became one of TBN's most popular personalities, and also joined the network's Board of Directors. Many Set Free faithful staffed TBN's 24-hour phone lines, counseling callers and taking donations.

The Bad Boy of California Evangelicals

As word spread and the crowds grew, Set Free was on its way to becoming of one of California's largest, most visible, and most unusual "mega-churches." Aguilar planted branches across the state, and deputized pastors, eventually growing his flock to about 4,000 members, over 300 of whom lived in the sect's houses. Many saw Aguilar's street-smart, informal style, and the growing network of Set Free ministries and homes, as a dynamic force that could rekindle Christian witness in late-1980s California.

But some local Christian leaders weren't enamored with Aguilar. Pastor Oden Fong of Costa Mesa's Calvary Chapel, whose own church had ministered to "Jesus Freak" hippies back in the day, often sent his church's most troubled members to Set Free houses for some Christian tough-love. But some returned, telling him that Aguilar cut them off from their families, micromanaged their social and romantic lives, and verbally or psychologically abused them. Fong himself thought that Aguilar's ministry, although passionate and hard-hitting, wasn't helping his new Christians mature into the faith, and instead just served the ex-con's own image as *The Bad Boy of California Evangelicals*.

The Calvary Chapel pastor distributed a flyer with the allegations about Aguilar to churches and civic groups across America. The flyer, and a controversial TV interview where Fong likened Aguilar to Peoples Temple suicide-cult leader Jim Jones, frightened religious organizations across California, and several Set Free ministries were shut down as a result. It also prompted a story in the *Orange County Register*, which corroborated the tales of abuse, and reported that Aguilar bought expensive cars and motorcycles for his own use, while most of his shelter-home faithful lived in dire poverty.

Outraged, Aguilar appealed to Chuck Smith, Fong's superior at Calvary Chapel, but the senior pastor refused to rein in his lieutenant. Aguilar also sent members of his Christian motorcycle club, Servants for Christ, to disrupt Fong's services, and unsuccessfully tried to sue him and another critical pastor. Set Free itself was named in two different lawsuits that alleged ministry leaders had physically and sexually abused some members; although the suits were settled amicably, the bad publicity cost Aguilar his TV show and board seat at Trinity Broadcasting Network.

Aguilar was also in trouble in Anaheim. Although city officials had initially praised Set Free's work, the home of Disneyland prided itself on its "family-friendly" environment, and feared the increasing influx of the scary-looking folks whom Aguilar ministered to and housed. In 1993 Set Free lost its lease on the

Fong likened Aguilar to Peoples Temple suicide-cult leader Jim Jones.

downtown warehouse-church; when it tried to relocate, city bureaucrats blocked Aguilar from setting up shop in three different locations. Finally, Aguilar tried to move Set Free headquarters to the Central Valley town of Visalia, but once again, he was stymied by local Christians and city officials concerned about his controversial ministry.

West Coast Flava

Burned out by the scandals and struggles, Aguilar took a sabbatical at the beachside community of Venice in West Los Angeles, where he preached to tourists and locals on the boardwalk. But the riot-scarred, gang-ridden City of the Angels was crying out for a major revival, and the erstwhile Orange County pastor reached out to TBN televangelist and Assembly of God preacher Tommy Barnett to help him build another urban ministry.

Aguilar and Barnett took over the massive, abandoned Queen of Angels hospital complex in downtown L.A., dubbed it The Dream Center, and dedicated themselves to ministering to inner-city youth, turning them away from drugs and the gang life, and onto Jesus. Aguilar's son Matthew formed a basketball league there, as well as a Christian rap group, Set Free (West Coast Flava) that toured high schools and youth centers in L.A.'s toughest neighborhoods, dropping hip-hop rhymes to praise the Lord.

Eventually Barnett and the Assemblies of God assumed full leadership of The Dream Center, and Aguilar returned to Anaheim. There, he reorganized his Servants for Christ motorcycle club as the Set Free Soldiers, choosing its toughest and most committed members as special evangelical envoys. The muscular, tattooed Harley riders worked Set Free's most challenging missionary field yet: outlaw-biker clubs like the Hells Angels, Mongols, and Vagos, whose turf-wars had claimed hundreds of lives across North America. Around this time the already heavily-tattooed Aguilar got a large, abstract swirl of black ink

Aguilar and wife Sandra
Credit: David Trotter

needled onto the left side of his face, when he figured he'd stepped too far outside mainstream society to ever seek a "normal" day job again.

As Aguilar described his mission years later to a reporter: "We go where a pizza man doesn't deliver. We get out there with the people on the highways and the byways of life. We tell them that if God took us, He'll take anybody." A memorable video made to promote the Soldiers showed a drunk derelict lying in a dark alleyway being approached by a hulking outlaw biker... who proceeds to witness Christ to the man, and promises to lead him to a new and better life.

Soldiers vs. Angels

Save for their club colors, the Set Free Soldiers were indistinguishable from other outlaw bikers, and Orange County police suspected Aguilar's Harley-riding evangelists were just another motorcycle gang bent on running contraband, fighting rivals, and raising hell throughout the region. Their suspicions were confirmed on July 27, 2008, when six Set Free Soldiers, including Aguilar and son Matthew, entered a bar, only to be confronted by several Hells Angels—members of the world's biggest and most feared biker club. The fight ended when a Soldier stabbed two Angels with a knife—an act that later earned him an eight-year prison sentence for attempted murder.

Although the Aguilars kept their distance during the brawl, and were let go afterwards by Newport Beach cops, they weren't off the police radar. Just before dawn on August 6, 2008, Aguilar awoke to the sounds of flash grenades, barking police dogs, rumbling armored cars, hovering helicopters, and loudspeaker commands, as over 150 rifle-toting lawmen from agencies across Southern California surrounded the compound where the Set Free leader lived with his extended family. "We saw a tank out front and all these SWAT-team guys," Aguilar later told journalist Nick Schou, "Brother, it was like the end of the world. I believe in the Rapture and all that stuff, and I thought this was the end thing of everything."

"We tell them that if God took us, He'll take anybody."

David Trotter

Set Free Soldiers

When Aguilar and his family surrendered, cops searched the whole Set Free compound. The shakedown produced naught but a single pistol, a set of brass knuckles, and one round of live ammunition in a coin jar by Aguilar's bed. For the police, that was enough to charge Aguilar, his son Matthew, and his son-in-law Michael Timanus with attempted murder, street terrorism, possession of deadly weapons by felons, and several other crimes.

Eventually the charges were dropped against Matthew, and ex-felon Timanus served seven months in jail for possession of a pistol. Aguilar's own case wasn't resolved until May 2010, when he pled guilty to being a felon in possession of ammunition, and got three years' informal probation. The Orange County District Attorney's office maintained that Christian or not, the Set Free Soldiers were still a criminal enterprise, and claimed that two club members had admitted as much in their plea agreements.

The busts and bad publicity not only fueled longstanding contentions that Aguilar was running a criminal gang under the guise of a Christian ministry, but it wrecked a lucrative deal Set Free had signed with the A&E cable network. A&E had advanced Aguilar a six-figure sum to tape a pilot episode for *Saint or Sinner,* a proposed reality-TV show that would examine the unconventional pastor's life and ministry from the inside. When news of the arrests hit the airwaves, the network cancelled the project.

Forty Years for "Pastor G"

> *"We saw a tank out front and all these SWAT-team guys… I thought this was the end of everything."*

Financially drained by the court battles, Aguilar reorganized Set Free Ministries after 2010. That year he also self-published a memoir, *Forgive Me Father for I Have Sinned,* that followed his journey from street-punk to prisoner to pastor, and pulled no punches regarding law enforcement, the City of Anaheim, rival Christian ministries, and other groups and individuals that plagued his work since the earliest days of the ministry. He continued to lead the Set Free Soldiers, and the tattooed biker-pastor remained a familiar, colorful figure in Southern California Evangelical circles, where he preached at both local Set Free ministries and at friendly churches.

Unfortunately for Aguilar, his troubles have continued as well. Many mainstream Christians continue to criticize Aguilar's approach, saying that Set Free's gangland/prison image glorifies a culture of intimidation and violence, and doesn't encourage its members to grow mentally or spiritually beyond the street-corner or the cell block. And some former followers, ex-residents of Set Free houses, and second-generation members who grew up inside the scene, continue to tell tales abuse by Aguilar and his lieutenants.

Once again, there was some ugly truth behind the allegations. In October 2015, a Texas court found Aguilar's 45 year-old son Geronimo guilty of sexual assault of children, and sentenced him to forty years in prison. Geronimo, who as "Pastor G" had led a Set Free branch in the Richmond, Virginia ghetto, had years earlier molested his then-11 and -13 year-old sisters-in-law during his time as a Fort Worth church-music director. Although devastated by the news, the elder Aguilar told reporters that he still loved his son, and would pray for him as he did for all the other sinners and criminals in Set Free's flock.

And Aguilar's ministry continues to this day, as an active—if scandal-plagued and offbeat—member of the Body of Christ. As he put it to a reporter, "The Church worldwide

David Trotter

Pastor Phil and Jonathan Davis of KORN

is like a big giant tossed salad, you got croutons, you got cucumbers. Set Free is like a little Tapatio hot sauce on top. Not many people put Tapatio on top of their salads, but the way the America [sic] is becoming, the mayo and mustard are going out."

16
Bishop Rodriguez
& the Mexican National Catholic Church

For many years, a small house-church in the East Los Angeles barrio was the final remnant of a once-sizable "Independent Catholic" Church that challenged the Vatican's domination of Mexican spiritual and cultural life.

The Mexican National Catholic Church arose in the wake of the 1910 Revolution, established scores of active parishes throughout both Mexico and the USA, became a viable rival to the Church of Rome, and eventually dwindled down to a single parish in California—only to be revived in the contempory American Southwest.

A Revolutionary "National Church"

From the day Cortez and his conquistadores set foot on the continent, the people of "New Spain" had always had an ambivalent relationship with the Roman Catholic Church. Although the passionate Iberian spiritual style had easily taken root in the New World, and Europe-

Bishop Emilio Rodriguez y Fairfield

Abbey of San Luigi

an, Indian, African, and *mestizo* peoples alike worshiped the bloody, suffering Hispanic Christ together under the benevolent gaze of the Virgin of Guadalupe, the Church itself had long been viewed by many as a symbol of Old World colonialism, and dominated by the Spanish *Criollo* establishment.

Over 1,400 priests were expelled from Mexico, and hundreds more were imprisoned or executed.

Long-simmering Mexican resentment against the Vatican finally boiled over in 1911 when revolutionaries overthrew Mexican dictator Porfirio Díaz. The insurgent government, which saw the Roman Catholic Church as an oppressive, foreign-run institution, assumed the power to license and authorize all religious activity in the nation. Six years later, the Constitution of 1917 banned the taking of religious vows, or the teaching of Christian doctrines in schools. Over the next decade the government seized all religious properties across Mexico, and thousands of churches, cathedrals, monasteries, and nunneries closed their doors.

Clerics as well were persecuted. Between 1924 and 1938 over 1,400 priests were expelled from Mexico, and hundreds more were imprisoned or executed. The 2,500-odd priests who remained at liberty disguised themselves and celebrated Mass in secret, while thousands of loyal Catholic peasants took up arms on their behalf against the government during the *Cristero* revolt of 1926-29.

Faced with both a popular rebellion and a resilient Roman Church, President Plutarco Elias Calles sought to establish a Mexican National Church that would meld Hispanic devotional fervor with nationalistic sentiment. The proposed Church would be free from Vatican and other foreign influences, would celebrate its liturgy in Spanish, and would kowtow to the secular government's wishes in all affairs temporal and spiritual.

To create such a Church, Calles looked to the so-called "Old Catholic" movement. The Old Catholics were European faithful whose clerics had dissented from the First Vatican Council of 1870, and broke with Rome to form independent communions in Germany, Austria and other countries. Although free from Papal control, these Churches, like the

Eastern Orthodox Patriarchates, were still recognized by the Holy See as having valid "Catholic" credentials, since their bishops could trace their authority, via a chain of episcopal consecration, to the original Apostles and Christ Himself.

"Old Catholic" Churches were independent of Rome, yet possessed valid apostolic authority.

The Old Catholic bishops in turn consecrated other prelates to the episcopal office, many of whom formed independent Catholic churches outside of Europe. One of these was Carmel Henry Carfora, an Italian immigrant and former Franciscan Capuchin priest who was made an Old Catholic bishop, and formed the North American Old Roman Catholic Church in 1916. Ten years later in Chicago, "Supreme Primate" Carfora consecrated former Roman priests Jose Joaquin Perez y Budar, Benicio Lopez Sierra, and Macario Lopez Valdes to the episcopacy, giving the fledgling Mexican National Church a hierarchy and a valid apostolic provenance.

CRISIS Magazine

Sr. Dn. Francisco Vera, anciano Sacerdote fusilado en Jalisco por celebrar la Santa Misa. 1927.

Mexican troops executing a Roman Catholic priest.

With the support of both President Calles and the Mexican government, newly-minted Bishop Perez established the *Iglesia Ortodoxa Catolica Apostolica Mexicana*. Known in English as the Mexican National Catholic Church, the new body featured Perez as Primate and Patriarch, while Lopez Sierra became his Coadjutor, and Lopez Valdes assumed the bishopric of Zaragoza. Perez also consecrated four additional bishops to oversee the Church in Hidalgo, Veracruz, Puebla and elsewhere. Later, Carfora would consecrate four more MNCC prelates.

The Mexico City Diocese of the MNCC joined the Orthodox Church in America in 1972.

With the Roman Church forced underground, thousands of Mexican Catholics turned to the National Church to receive the sacraments and accept spiritual guidance. But there was no real unity among the schismatic bishops, and they fought each other over Church doctrine and practices, as well as the Vatican for dominance in the hearts and minds of their flocks. The septuagenarian Patriarch was too old and frail to enforce discipline in his episcopal ranks, and he eventually gave up, reconciling himself to the Holy See before his death in 1931.

Perez' successor was young Eduardo Davila-Garcia, who had been ordained an MNCC priest at the age of eighteen. A Mexican nationalist and a Freemason, Garcia was consecrated a bishop in 1933, and held the self-titled position of *Eduardo Primo, primer papa de Mexico* until 1938, when he left the church. He was replaced by Joseph Petrus Ortiz, who in turn yielded his Patriarchate to Armin Monte de Honor in 1958.

As the years passed, and the passions of the Revolution and the *Cristero* Rebellion gradually

Rafael de la Cova

Mexican Cristero rebels

faded, relations between the Roman Church and the Mexican State thawed considerably. After the Vatican paid reparations for its losing role in the Revolution, the government invited the exiled Roman clergy to return to their old positions, and reoccupy all the vacant cathedrals and churches.

For 50 years Bishop Rodriguez led the MNCC out of his house in East Los Angeles.

The Mexican National Catholic Church, with a mere 120 priests and parishes spread across fourteen Mexican states, found it difficult to compete with the re-legalized, resurgent Church of Rome. From 1940 onwards it steadily lost membership and influence, and also found itself on the receiving end of scorn as a living symbol of the Revolution's anticlerical excesses. The final blow came in 1972 when the last major center of National Church activity—the Mexico City Diocese—was absorbed into the Orthodox Church in America, with its Patriarch Jose Cortes y Olmas donning Eastern Christian vestments and assuming the title of Exarch.

The MNCC in Alta California

Ironically enough, the Mexican National Catholic Church lived on not in Mexico itself, but in the land that had annexed so much of its old territory, and housed millions of its economic and political exiles. Although the Church had boasted a presence in the United States since 1929, when Bishop Carfora consecrated a Hieronymus Maria to head up a San Antonio, Texas-based diocese, the MNCC's most solid stronghold in *Yanqui* territory was in Los Angeles.

Back in 1926, on a visit to relatives in Southern California, MNCC Bishop Macario Lopez y Valdes met Bishop Roberto T. Gonzalez, a former Church of the Nazarene pastor and the leader of *El Hogar de la Verdad*, a Spiritualist church that ministered to East Los Angeles' Mexican-American community. Despite their ostensible theological differences, the two prelates became friends, and Lopez y Valdez consecrated Gonzalez to the episcopate, and appointed him to be the Bishop of the MNCC in East Los Angeles.

MNCC/John Parnell

MNCC Coat of Arms

After Gonzalez passed on in 1928, Lopez y Valdez consecrated his successor, Alberto Luis Rodriguez y Durand, as the MNCC Bishop Ordinary of Los Angeles, and Regionary Bishop of *Alta California*. As a result, *El Hogar de la Verdad* became "The Old Catholic Orthodox Church of St. Augustine of the Mystical Body of Christ," and the center of MNCC activity in the American State.

Assisting Bishop Rodriguez y Durand with the parish was his younger brother, Emile Federico Rodriguez. A former Olympic athlete who had represented Mexico in the 1932 Games' 1500-meter race, the younger Rodriguez was ordained to the priesthood in 1938 by his brother. He then migrated to Los Angeles, became an American citizen, found work as a physical-education instructor, and added "Fairfield" to his surname in 1953 as both a concession to his new home's *Anglo* culture, and as a poetic tribute to his prowess on the track.

In 1955, Rodriguez y Fairfield received episcopal consecration from his ailing older brother, and took over as the head of the Church in California. For the next 50 years he shepherded an estimated 100 Mexican and Mexican-American parishioners out of his little house-church at 4011 East Brooklyn (now Cesar Chavez) Avenue in East Los Angeles. As the MNCC faded from view in Mexico itself, the Bishop and his mostly-Californian flock remained faithful to the vision of a Spanish-speaking, non-Eurocentric, and independent Catholic Church.

When Bishop Jose Cortes y Olmos died in Mexico in 1983, Bishop Rodriguez became the last living Bishop of the MNCC, and was named its Archbishop and Primate. By this time the East Los Angeles prelate had become something of a celebrity in the world of independent Catholicism, and divided his time between the MNCC's last parish, and the Old Roman Catholic Church/ Canonical Old Roman Catholic Church, a mostly-Anglo independent body that he had assumed leadership of in 1982.

"We're like the Amish, except we'll drink and fight and cuss!"

In the manner of so many other "Wandering Bishops," Rodriguez also swapped apostolic pedigrees with his fellow prelates, receiving further consecrations from leaders of such bodies and passing his own lines of succession along to other would-be episcopates. The 77 year-old Bishop briefly made national headlines in 1990 when he and two other independent bishops raised married Roman Catholic priest George A. Stallings, Jr. to the episcopacy, and enabled the controversial cleric to found and head his own African-American Catholic Congregation as yet another ethnic/nationalist schism from the Holy See.

Perhaps Rodriguez' most significant secondary consecration was from Bishop Francisco Pagtakhan of the Philippine Independent Catholic Church, a schismatic body with an anti-colonial and nationalistic history similar to the MNCC's. The Mexican patriarch also established intercommunion between the MNCC and the considerably larger Filipino church, and brought into his orbit dissident Lutheran and Roman Catholic clerics who had affiliated with the PICC.

Patriarch John Parnell

by permission of John Parnell

Revival in Tejas

When the aging Bishop Rodriguez finally passed on in 2005, the helm of the Mexican National Catholic Church fell to a most unusual, dynamic and—most significantly—*non-Mexican* man. Texan John Parnell, who had received episcopal consecration from Philippine Independent Catholic Church bishops, planted a fresh MNCC parish in his home town of Fort Worth, and set about turning the Church from an obscure remnant of Mexican Catholic history, into an active and vibrant spiritual force in East Texas' Mexican-American community.

Calling his parish "Saint Augustine's Catholic Church," Bishop Parnell created a Catholic community that more resembled the frontier Spanish missions of pre-Alamo *Tejas*, than it did a contemporary Roman Catholic parish. An episode of the *Texas Country Reporter* news program showed Parnell and his parishioners tending livestock, tilling soil, repairing boots, and rolling cigars on the Church properties like something out of an Old West living-history panorama. When reporter Bob Phillips said that their no-frills lifestyle reminded him of the Amish, Parnell joked, "We're like the Amish, except we'll drink and fight and cuss!"

Humor aside, Bishop Parnell sought to create a Church and community that preserved the old ways of Spanish and Mexican Texas. Along with the farming and craft activities, he founded the St. Augustine Catholic School, which taught dozens of trades and life-skills to impoverished Fort Worth residents. And the small local church carried on the MNCC's traditions with its quaint Hispanic iconography, its distinctly Mexican-flavored liturgy of Spanish language and folk-music, and its proud independence from Rome.

Parnell's work made him something of a local media figure in Fort Worth, and he networked extensively with other Independent Catholic bishops and churches. Parnell also planted a new MNCC parish in Los Angeles—the city where his predecessor Bishop Rodriguez tended the last spark of the once-fiery spiritual movement for so many years.

It may seem ironic that a Mexican-nationalist denomination was long preserved, and is being revived, in the land of its Northern rival. But as the cultural, economic and political boundaries between Mexico and the United States blur ever more, there will be more intersection of the two nations' distinct spiritual traditions. In the current Mexican National Catholic Church one can see both the history and culture of the deeply-Catholic yet fiercely-patriotic Hispanic world, and the proudly independent and entrepreneurial spirit of North American frontier individualism. Although Bishop Parnell and others acknowledge the MNCC as "a piece of living history," it also points towards a future where the two countries' spiritual and social ways are ever more entwined and melded.

17

Mel Gibson
& the Church of the Holy Family

While the Mexican National Catholic Church represents the progressive/ethnic-pride wing of independent Catholicism in California, Malibu's Church of the Holy Family symbolizes a very different form of that ecclesiastic subculture.

The Church of the Holy Family is the state's most famous "Catholic traditionalist" parish, largely because of its association with Mel Gibson—one of the world's most famous and controversial movie stars. The small, secretive group preaches and practices an ultra-orthodox, pre-Modernist form of Roman doctrine and worship that it believes makes its faithful *literally* more Catholic than the Pope.

Revolt Against Vatican II

So-called Catholic Traditionalist groups emerged in the wake of the Second Vatican Council of 1965. In the years after that Council, the Old Catholic

Georges Biard

Mel Gibson: a Catholic Traditionalist

controversy of a century earlier seemed to repeat itself, as many Roman Catholic clergy and laity objected to Vatican II's sweeping liturgical and doctrinal changes—especially the new mandate to pray the Mass in the local vernacular, rather than Latin. Although most Catholics accepted the Papal *Novus Ordo*, some formed schismatic groups that celebrated the old Latin Mass and adhered to pre-1960s teachings and usages.

Like the Old Catholics, the traditionalist groups saw themselves as not as schismatic rebels, but as purists holding out against the false teachings and heresy of a corrupted Church. One group, Archbishop Marcel Lefebvre's Society of St. Pius X, became a sizable international movement, with hundreds of trained clergy, and scores of chapels, seminaries, and retreats where the Latin Tridentine Rite was celebrated, women wore head coverings in church, fish was eaten on Fridays, and Rome's pre-Vatican II doctrines were immutable, unquestioned Truth.

At least four non-Vatican "Catholic Popes" exist.

Although the Society continued to pray for the Pope and for the return of the old liturgies and doctrines, other schismatic groups—the "sedevacantist" (empty seat) faction—believed that no Pope since John XXIII had any claim on legitimacy, and actively opposed his successors. A few Traditionalist sects even elected their own Popes—at present, at least four known claimants to the Papal throne exist in such disparate places as Spain, Kansas, and Australia.

The Passion of Mel Gibson

The Church of the Holy Family is one of the world's best-known Traditionalist movements. Its single parish celebrates the Latin Mass in an attractive, Spanish-style chapel that sits on a 16-acre plot in the brushy Santa Monica Mountains, about six miles' north of Malibu. Only about 70 parishioners attend this church, which is closed to the general public.

The Church of the Holy Family formed when a Traditionalist parish in San Gabriel was absorbed by the Society of St. Pius X, and several families left in protest of the new leadership. They formed an even smaller schismatic group that started constructing its own church building in the mountains around 2002.

Gibson called the Holy See "a wolf in sheep's clothing".

Holy Family might have gone unnoticed by all but keen observers of the Catholic-traditionalist world had it not been for an article in the March 9, 2003 *New York Times Magazine*. In that piece, writer Christopher Noxon revealed that the person who was financing the church-building project was none other than Mel Gibson, the ruggedly handsome and devoutly Catholic Australian-American star of *Braveheart*, and the *Mad Max* and *Lethal Weapon* movies.

Gibson, who as a happily-married father of seven was something of an anomaly in the libertine film business, hadn't exactly kept his Tridentine tendencies a secret. He told *USA Today* in a 2001 interview that he attended "an all-pre-Vatican II Latin Mass," and also made "a scathing attack against the Vatican" in the Italian newspaper *Il Giornale*, calling the Holy See "a wolf in sheep's clothing." But Noxon's article revealed that Gibson took a far more active role in the Traditionalist movement, forming and heading a nonprofit corporation that funneled millions of dollars to the Holy Family building construction.

Holy Family got an even bigger injection of development capital in the wake of *The Passion of the Christ*, the controversial blockbuster movie that Gibson co-wrote, co-produced, and directed. Independently financed and distributed, cast largely with unknown actors, and with its dialogue entirely in Latin, Hebrew, and Aramaic, *The Passion* retold the events of Jesus' last twelve hours before the Crucifixion from a distinctly pre-Vatican II Catholic perspective that emphasized

Giuseppi Felici

Catholic Traditionalist hero: Pope St. Pius X

His bloody tortures and sufferings. Although it was criticized as being historically inaccurate, and accused of using anti-Semitic imagery and themes, the movie grossed an astonishing $611 million in worldwide release, with much of the take going straight back to Gibson.

Gibson's father claimed that Vatican II was "a Masonic plot backed by the Jews".

The charges about the film's alleged anti-Semitism gained credence when Gibson's father, the octogenarian Hutton Gibson, began talking to mainstream reporters. A famed Catholic Traditionalist and sedevacantist who had been attacking the "false Popes" in books and articles since the late Sixties, *pere* Gibson told Noxon and other writers that the Second Vatican Council was "a Masonic plot backed by the Jews," and denied that the Holocaust had ever occurred. Although the movie star distanced himself from his father's more rash statements, many wondered if Mel himself privately shared Hutton's uglier beliefs, especially in the wake of a 2006 arrest for drunken driving, in which the film star apparently said to one of the arresting officers, "Fucking Jews....Jews are responsible for all the wars in the world. Are you a Jew?" Although he publically apologized for his outburst, and sought help for what he said was a lifelong drinking problem, hurt feelings and skepticism remained.

Still, Mel Gibson pressed on with the Church. In 2008 it was revealed that the A.P. Reilly Foundation, the nonprofit corporation that controlled and subsidized the Church, held a whopping $42 million in assets. A year earlier, the Church building was consecrated by Archbishop Emeritus Carlos Quintero Arce

Fanciful depiction of the Latin Mass.

of Hermosillo, Mexico, who also confirmed the actor's grandchildren months later. The presence of a legitimate, albeit retired, Roman Catholic prelate at the chapel seemed to confirm that Gibson hadn't really distanced himself all that much from the Holy See, although some observers speculated that the octogenarian Quintero Arce had been chosen since his episcopal status predated Vatican II.

Traditionalists and Aquarians

Oddly enough, the ultra-orthodox Holy Family Church shared common ground—literally—with one of California's more exotic spiritual orders. A Fox News reporter revealed that in 1999, the A.P. Reilly Foundation spent nearly $1.4 million to purchase a plot of land adjacent to the church site from a sect called the Aquarian Educational Group.

The Aquarian Educational Group is a Theosophical religious and educational organization founded by Torkom Saraydarian (1917-1997), an Armenian immigrant and author of many books that explored the teachings of H.P. Blavatsky, Alice Bailey, Helena Roerich, and other purveyors of occult wisdom that would horrify most Traditionalist Catholics. Appropriately enough, Saraydarian, who had once studied for the Armenian Orthodox priesthood, was also a bishop in the Independent Church of Antioch—a sect that combined Catholic liturgy and Christian worship with esoteric and neo-Gnostic doctrines.

Since then, the Church of the Holy Family has maintained a low profile, rarely mentioned in the media, and then only in connection with Mel Gibson's doings. His daughter Hannah, who had reportedly once considered becoming a nun, married blues guitarist Kenny Wayne Shepherd at the church in a ceremony on September 17, 2006.

Three years later, Gibson raised Traditionalist eyebrows when he divorced his wife—a major no-no in orthodox Catholic doctrine—and took up with a Russian pianist, with whom he had a daughter out of wedlock. Eventually Gibson split with her as well, and the legal settlements with her and his ex-wife Robyn cost him dearly, and drastically cut his sponsorship of Holy Family. Still, the parish exists to this day, its gated grounds patrolled by security guards and its Sunday services closed to all but a few dozen pre-screened faithful.

It's tempting to dismiss Holy Family, the MNCC, or the myriad of other independent-Catholic sects, as inconsequential fringe-phenomena—play-churches dreamed up by people too quixotic or querulous to submit to the discipline of the historic Roman Church, yet desiring the legitimacy associated with this largest and most ancient of Christian denominations. But many of the issues the independents raise, whether regarding Church-State relations, liturgy, the historical doctrines, or the true meaning of the Christian faith, are quite valid, and may not be adequately addressed by the Vatican's one-size-fits-all approach.

Whether their founders be movie stars, Mexican revolutionaries, or ordinary Christians, the independent Catholic sects will be part of the Californian and global spiritual landscape for a long time.

18
Leonard Knight
& Salvation Mountain

One hundred miles east of San Diego, in the flat, sub-sea level desert near the town of Niland, stands a huge, multicolored monument to one man's faith that might be the most quintessentially Californian of all Christian witnesses.

Called "Salvation Mountain," this gargantuan piece of folk-devotional art is a sprawling manmade hill of adobe, straw, and paint, festooned with brightly-colored Biblical verses and affirmations of God's love, and topped with a wooden cross. For many years the Mountain was an obscure local curiosity, until it was discovered by travel writers, art critics, and the mass-media, and this towering product of over 30 years of one man's labor gained a worldwide audience.

Salvation Mountain

Judith Rosenberg

A Sinner's Prayer

The one man was Leonard Clark Knight. Born in in 1931, Knight was a high-school

Knight attempted to build a hot-air balloon bearing the words "GOD IS LOVE".

dropout and Korean War veteran who worked as a car-painter and guitar-teacher in his native Vermont. Although he'd had no interest in religion or Jesus growing up, during a 1967 visit to San Diego Knight suddenly started reciting the Sinner's Prayer—"Jesus, I'm a sinner, please come upon my body and into my heart"—and received Christ as his Lord and Savior.

Knight returned to Vermont, but discovered that his newfound fervor was unwelcome in the orthodox Christian churches he visited. When he insisted that Christ simply wanted us to accept Him in our hearts, repent of our sins, and be saved, churchmen rebuked him as ignorant and naïve.

But Knight persisted, hoping to find a medium and an audience for his message of God's love. When a hot-air balloon emblazoned with words floated over Burlington in 1970, Knight thought he'd found a perfect way to spread the Word to the masses, and prayed that he'd get an opportunity to decorate and pilot such a craft. Eventually he realized he had to construct his own Gospel-balloon, and in 1980 he started gathering strips of fabric, using a second-hand sewing machine to piece them together around a big white canvas that read "GOD IS LOVE" in red letters. But he was unable to successfully inflate the balloon, and its fabric began to fade and rot.

Disheartened, and tired of Vermont's chilly temperatures and attitudes, Knight went West once more. One day he found himself in the town of Niland, California, near the shores of the Salton Sea. Knight liked the dry, endless-summer climate of the

Joe Decruyenaere

Leonard Knight

low desert, and camped out in his van on the vast tract of public land just outside of town, still hoping to somehow spread his message of God's love to the world.

Over 100,000 gallons of paint have been applied to Salvation Mountain.

With his balloon project literally in tatters, Knight prepared to hit the road once more. But he wanted to make one final gesture, and leave a small, permanent monument to his faith in the state where he'd found God. So he chose a spot by a dry riverbank, bought a sack of cement and some paint, and gave himself one week to erect a pillar painted with Christian slogans—a smaller, terrestrial version of the Gospel balloon he'd dreamed of floating across America.

But the week became a month, the month became a year, and year after year passed by as Knight settled into his Niland camp, grew obsessed with the monument, and worked from dawn to dusk on it. To build the structure, Knight mixed together desert sand and debris from a nearby dump, covered it with a layer of cement, and painted the dry surface with the same bright colors he'd favored for his balloon.

After about four years of work, the monument grew to over fifty feet in height. At its front and center was the familiar "GOD IS LOVE" slogan in huge red letters on a white field. Below that were the words of the "Sinner's Prayer," with a big red heart at the base, and colorful lines, swirls, and abstract patterns along the sides. Unfortunately, the cement-sand-rubble matrix proved to be unstable, and the manmade mountain collapsed in 1989.

Adobe, Straw, and Paint

Undaunted, Knight took its fall as a sign from God that he needed to find a stronger and more permanent medium for construction. He decided that native adobe clay mixed with straw would work best in the desert environment, and began to rebuild the monument that would soon be known as "Salvation Mountain." Knight found that covering the dried adobe with coats of paint added extra layers of protection against the elements, and it's estimated that over 100,000 gallons of lead-free paint have been applied to the mountain as sealant and decoration.

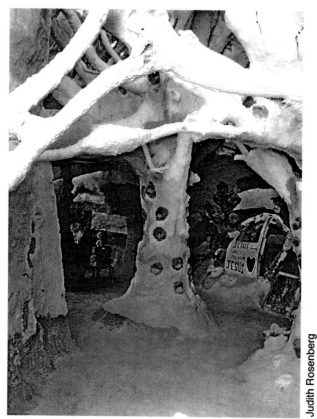

Interior of Salvation Mountain's "Museum"

During the 1990s, Salvation Mountain grew to over 50 feet in height and 150 feet in width. The "GOD IS LOVE" motto now topped its crest in three-dimensional red letters, and below it was a huge red heart emblazoned with the "Sinner's Prayer" in stark white text. A riot of colors covered other parts of the Mountain with Biblical verses, an American flag, rainbows, trees, birds, flowers, hearts, sunbursts, and all sorts of abstract patterns. At its base was Knight's depiction of the Sea of Galilee.

Knight, who lived out of a gypsy wagon-like truck in the Mountain's shadow, continued to build and paint the adobe knoll even in the punishing desert heat, when summer temperatures could easily reach 120°F or more. His efforts were supplemented by a small but steadily increasing stream of visitors to the Mountain, who donated cans of paint and other supplies, and marveled over the gargantuan, multicolored testimony to faith in the middle of one of the Western Hemisphere's bleakest deserts. Many of the visitors came from nearby "Slab City," a community of trailer- and shack-dwelling "snowbirds" and social-dropouts who squatted on the former site of Fort Dunlap, a World War II training base.

The "Slabs," as the residents were known locally, frustrated cash-strapped Imperial County officials, who couldn't collect taxes or rents from the Federal-land squatters. Seeking to have both Slab City and Salvation Mountain condemned, in July 1994 the County sent out a toxic-waste specialist to the Mountain, who took soil samples from around it and immediately proclaimed the area a "toxic nightmare." When the County petitioned the State of California for funds to tear down the Mountain and haul it away to a toxic-waste dump, Knight hired an independent consultant to test soil from the same spots the specialist had sampled. When the test came up negative for contaminants, the County dropped its plans.

"Jesus is Beautiful and Pretty"

As the decade wore on, Knight continued to build, improve, and expand the Mountain. In 1998 he constructed "The Hogan": a domed room with a ten-foot high ceiling that shaded him and his visitors from the harsh desert sun. Knight built steps, benches, and a small mezzanine into the room, and decorated its adobe walls with sky-blue paint, and scores of little "paintings" that depicted clouds, green fields, sunrises, flowers, trees, and birds, or sported slogans like "ACTS 2:38 BIBLE GOD IS LOVE" and "ALL PEOPLE YOU ARE LOVED." The Hogan also housed several trophies that Knight won for his "art cars": his truck, an old trailer, and a couple of other vehicles on the property that were covered with multicolored designs and writing similar to the ones on the Mountain.

By the 21st Century Knight was also working on "The Museum." This was a large, vaulted room honeycombed with tunnels and alcoves, lit from the ceiling with salvaged car-windows, and pillared with bare-limbed "trees" he'd made of adobe and landfill junk. Knight decorated the Museum with more of the Mountain's wild colors, primitive drawings, and Christian sayings, and saw it as a concave, earthbound answer to the balloon he'd never successfully launched.

Eventually, stories of the huge, colorful Christian art-project and its gentle, hardworking creator made their way outside of Slab City and Niland. In 1996 television host Huell Howser dedicated an episode of his *California Gold* show to Knight and the Mountain; six years later Peter Jennings featured them on *World News Tonight*. Music videos were shot at the site, with the Mountain creating a colorful, bizarre backdrop for artists' performances. And in 2002 US Senator Barbara Boxer also read a tribute to Knight and the Mountain into the *Congressional Record*.

Knight and Salvation Mountain were formally honored by the U.S. Senate.

Dozens of newspaper and magazine stories profiled the man and his work, and cultural observers saw the Mountain as perhaps the world's
biggest piece of folk or "primitive" art. A full-length
book—Sara Patterson's *Middle of Nowhere: Religion, Art,
and Pop Culture at Salvation Mountain*—made the case
that Knight was not only a unique devotional artist, but a modern-day equivalent of the
Christian faith's early desert prophets and ascetics who received and instructed pilgrims in
their wilderness retreats.

*Knight starred as himself in the movie **Into the Wild.***

Knight himself modestly denied that he was an "artist," and saw himself as nothing
more than a humble evangelist who spread the Good News with paint and adobe rather than printed words or broadcasts, and who spurned doctrinaire teachings in favor of
earnest affirmations. As he told writer Joe Oesterle, "I just want to prove to the people
that God is love. It says so in the Bible… And if the holy Bible says something, I believe
it." Knight refused to speak of hellfire-and-damnation; as he saw it, "Jesus is beautiful and
pretty, and we should be comfortable talking about God's love and the prettiness of God."
The Mountain was how he communicated that beauty to the world.

The desert-dwelling loner was even featured in a major Hollywood movie. The 2007
biopic *Into the Wild* included a scene where ill-fated adventurer Christopher McCandless,
played by Emile Hirsch, visits Salvation Mountain. The white-haired, leather-skinned
Knight played himself in the scene, showing Hirsch and costar Kristen Stewart around the
Mountain, telling them about God's love, and insisting he wouldn't leave his simple life on
the desert "for ten million dollars."

Ashes to Ashes

Throughout the 2000s Knight continued to work on the Mountain and receive visitors—
sometimes as many as 100 a day during the cooler winter months. But around the time
of his 80th birthday his health began to decline, and in late 2011 he entered a convalescent
hospital in eastern San Diego County, suffering from the ravages of diabetes and the onset
of senile dementia. In his absence, volunteers maintained the Mountain.

Finally, on February 10, 2014, Leonard Knight passed over to meet the Lord whose love he had proclaimed for the better part of his 82 years. His remains were cremated; part of his ashes were interred at Fort Rosecrans National Cemetery, while the rest were scattered over the towering monument he'd raised from the floor of the Salton Sea desert.

Today, a nonprofit corporation, Salvation Mountain Inc. maintains the mountain. The organization raises money, recruits caretakers and docents, and organizes work parties to help preserve the huge, unique piece of Christian devotional art. Although part of the corporation's mission is "to spread the message that God loves everyone to the world and to have hate vanish as love takes over," its ranks include secularists who see in the life and work of Knight a tribute to the human spirit and its endless potential for creativity and compassion.

The author at Salvation Mountain

To this day, the visitors continue to travel along the Salton Sea shores, down Highway 111 to 601 East Beal Road, where the Mountain stands. Many of them climb the adobe stairs to the top of Salvation Mountain to view the vast desert panorama. Others photograph the artwork that adorns the Mountain, the Hogan, the Museum, and the various abandoned vehicles, marveling at Knight's simple dedication and vision. Some find their way to the ramshackle "visitor center," and leave dedications in its weather-beaten guestbook, or drop bills in its colorfully-painted donations box.

And a few pilgrims to the Mountain meditate on the simple, direct message that Knight painted on it in words and pictures: that God loves every one of us, speaks to us in both His Creation and in Scripture, and urges us to turn away from sin and accept Him into our hearts. To them, Salvation Mountain is not just a roadside curiosity or a bizarre, epic-sized folk-art relic, but a pure and sincere public expression of faith, and mute testimony to the often eccentric—but always heartfelt—fervor that has characterized Californian Christian spirituality from the state's earliest days.

About the Author

Mike Marinacci's fascination with the California's unique history and culture evolved into *California Jesus*. He is the author of *Mysterious California*, and the bestselling *Weird California*.

As a scholar of religious history and sociology, Mr. Marinacci has focused on American spiritual groups and leaders, especially the unorthodox sects and figures who have emerged from the Golden State.

Mr. Marinacci provides keynotes and consults on California's Sects, Evangelists and Latter-Day Prophets. He resides in the San Francisco Bay Area.

For more information, contact: mikal9000@gmail.com.

RO-NIN
Ro = *wave;* **nin** = *man*

Books for Independent Minds

**Visit roninpub.com
Enjoy!
Use isbn to order from
a local bookstore,
Amazon, or other
online outlet.**

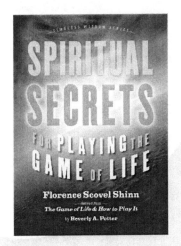

CPSIA information can be obtained at www.ICGtesting.com
Printed in the USA
LVOW09s2344131016

508602LV00002B/8/P

9 781579 512309